VINTAGE
GRAND RAPIDS
A KALEIDOSCOPE OF PHOTOGRAPHS Vol. II

Published by

THE GRAND RAPIDS
PRESS
Be someone who gets it.

Danny R. Gaydou, Publisher

Copyright 2008. All rights reserved.
Printed in Canada
ISBN 978-0-9785053-2-5

PREFACE

The rich history of Grand Rapids lives in every resident who calls the area home. The photos in this book, shared by you, are snapshots of times and places gone by; nostalgic glimpses of the river of history that flows through our lives. Through them, we are enriched as we recall the memories they evoke. We remember the traditions that were laid down before us and are cherished by us today. We also smile at the well-remembered faces, the mischievous looks on the schoolchildren we once were, the soda fountain where we took our first date or the soldier who went to war on our behalf. This is our family scrapbook, the scrapbook of Grand Rapids; photos of the people we were who helped to make who we are now. We are very proud to share this second volume of Vintage Grand Rapids with you. Enjoy.

James Davis
Editor, Vintage Grand Rapids
Volume II

With the North Park Pavilion on the far shore, two well-dressed men are found rafting on the Grand River in this 1920s-era photo. Chas Kunze, left, has hung his coat from a peg on the shanty and is enjoying a pipe. His raft-mate, Emil Reichel, still has his coat on. Were they engineers surveying the riverbank or two latter-day Huck Finns? Not much else is known about this photo from the Grand Rapids Public Library collection other than the rather leisurely mystery it presents. *PHOTO/Courtesy Grand Rapids Public Library*

Cover Photo: City buses replace street cars in this late 1940s-era street scene looking southeast on Monroe Street at the Pearl Street intersection.

PHOTO/Courtesy Grand Rapids City Archives

ACKNOWLEDGMENTS

Vintage Grand Rapids Vol. II

Project Staff

Sheri Stetson-Compton – Project Director
James Davis – Editor
Jeanne Vaughn – Project Assistant
Lindsey Willey – Editorial Intern
Todd Vander Wal – Layout/Design
Dave Hayden – Marketing
Debra Richmond – Clerical Assistant
Debra Novak – Production
Anne Kasianowicz – Photo Editing
Dan Johnson, Duane Stick – Photo Technicians
Mary Jo Hills, Todd Michalski, Christine Mwanyika – Database Support
Dave Arbanas, Linda Bolt, Wilma Richardson, Melanie Vandekerkhoff,
Dave Vida, Laurie Deyer – Accounting Support
Jan Ringler – Customer Service Support

Special thanks to

Grand Rapids Public Library
Kristen Krueger-Corrado, Marketing and Communications Manager
Tim Gleisner, Manager, Grand Rapids History & Special Collections
Chris Byron, Grand Rapids History & Special Collections
Rebecca Mayne, Librarian Specialist Archives
Jennifer Morrison, Grand Rapids History & Special Collections
Karolee Hazlewood, Grand Rapids History & Special Collections

Grand Rapids City Archives, William Cunningham

Public Museum of Grand Rapids, Veronica L. Kandl, Curator

Peter M. Wege

INTRODUCTION

The photographs in this book could be from our family's scrapbook as they could be from your family's—if you were lucky enough to grow up in Grand Rapids. My father Peter M. Wege came here to found Metal Office Furniture (now Steelcase) in 1912. He married a Grand Rapids girl from the West Side, Sophia Louise Dubridge, and I was born in their first home on South Division in 1920. As you browse these wonderful old photographs from the 1800s to the 1960s, you will see your own family's story reflected here as well. This book renews my pride in the best city I know. I've traveled all over the world, but I am always happy to get back to my home town.

Enjoy Vintage Grand Rapids.

Peter M. Wege

Peter Martin Wege and his wife, Sophia Louise (Dubridge), stand in front of their home at 2630 Lake Drive SE in East Grand Rapids. The couple wed in 1917 when Peter was 47 and Sophia was 32. Their only child, Peter Melvin, was born on Feb. 19, 1920. The elder Peter Wege founded the Metal Office Furniture Company in 1912. In December 1954, the company would be renamed Steelcase Inc.

1800s

Right around 1884, the Julius J. Wagner Groceries & Provisions store on 197 E. Bridge St. at Lafayette Avenue offered a handsome variety of goods for local folk. You could also get feed and hay for the animals in your life. They'd deliver, too, via the horsedrawn wagons seen on both sides of the photo. In the doorway are Julius J. Wagner, left, Minnie S. Wagner and Edward L. Wagner. *PHOTO/Courtesy John R. Wagner*

Four children of John Rauser, owner of a sausage factory on Bridge Street NW, are shown in this 1895 photo. Clockwise from top left: Otto, John, Tillie and Emma.

PHOTO/Courtesy S.J. King

William T. Powers, far left, is shown with his family in 1869. Powers was mayor of Grand Rapids in 1869 and had the honor of bringing in the first water-powered furniture factory, the first plate glass windows on his showroom building and electric street lighting to the city. In fact, that hydro-electric power generation was the first of its kind in the nation. The west side power canal was built to harness this power and is largely the reason the city is where it is today. Mary Ann Powers, second from right, was active in the suffrage movement and a close friend of Susan B. Anthony.

PHOTO/Courtesy James R. Winslow

Immanuel Lutheran Church is shown around 1890, shortly after its completion on Bridge Street (now Michigan) at Division Avenue. Cobblestones, a rail line in the center of the street and hitching posts have given way to several new health facilities on Michigan Street's "Medical Mile," but the church is still there.

PHOTO/Courtesy Immanuel Lutheran Church

Triplets born to Fred and Mrs. Esweiner in July 1897 became but fraternal twins just four days after their birth. William, the middle infant, was too weak to live. His sister, Edna, left, and Edmund, survived. This photo was taken one day before William's death. A newspaper of the time devoted a column to the tragedy, noting that, in a strange turn, visitors were admitted for a fee to see the two living children and the one deceased. Money collected went to help the "industrious, but quite poor," parents.

PHOTO/Courtesy Julie Esenwein Zinderman

Grand Rapids has produced its share of notoriety. Mary Allen Hulbert Peck, shown here in the 1880s, was born on Bridge Street in Grand Rapids. The granddaughter of Dr. Sterling Way Allen, she wed scientist Thomas Hulbert, heir to a copper mine fortune. She became a world traveler and socialite, and was called a robust conversationalist who moved easily in high social circles. Some reports also picture her as shallow and vain. In Bermuda in the early 1900s, she befriended novelist Mark Twain and met future U.S. President Woodrow Wilson, with whom she later shared a controversial relationship during his presidency. She later became an interior decorator, living in Manhattan.

PHOTO/Courtesy Ron Strauss

Theresa Eules Loibl was an early immigrant to Grand Rapids. She sat for a studio portrait with her four children – Mary, Teresa, Sophia and Anthony – in 1897.

PHOTO/Courtesy Kathy Sloane Wortman

The young military man with the sad eyes is Rufus Boer, who was with the 32 Regiment, Michigan Volunteers Infantry Co. E in 1898 when the call to duty came to serve in the Spanish American War. The lads were just about to embark for Cuba when hostilities ceased and the 32nd returned home, resumed its 2nd Infantry designation and moved into a new armory. Rufus was a member of the Guy V. Henry Post, Camp 3. He resided at 236 Carroll Ave. SE and is buried in Oakhill Cemetery.

PHOTO/Courtesy John R. Wagner

These two winsome chaps are Louis, left, and William Zandbergen, who were the sons of Bert and Nellie (Huizenga) Zandbergen. The family farmed land in the Grandville area. The two lads were posed sometime around 1894-95.

PHOTO/Courtesy Gary and Bette Zandbergen

Just around 1890, Peck's Drug Store had a good corner to do business. It was Monroe Avenue (now Monroe Center) and Division Avenue. If the price of gas keeps rising, will the horse and buggy come back? *PHOTO/Courtesy Joanne Keenan*

Peter Stark looked the part of a Western hombre, but he was delivering milk and cream in the "brickyard" area of Fulton Street and Diamond Avenue around 1890 in this photo. Stark was on his route for about 30 years, according to his grandson, Bernard.

PHOTO/Courtesy Bernard Stark

These ladies obliged a photographer in 1895. Far left is Ella Carpenter, great aunt of Sister Michael Ellen Carling.

PHOTO/Courtesy Sister Michael Ellen Carling

In the mid 1880s, Wagner & Clark delivered groceries and other provisions to its customers via this sturdy conveyance. The store was on Bridge Street at Lafayette Avenue, approximately where the Cook Institute now stands on Michigan Street hill.

PHOTO/Courtesy John R. Wagner

An 1895 scene captures a quiet downtown street near the Majestic Theater on Division Avenue. The building is now part of the Meijer Majestic Civic Theater. The photo was reproduced from a glass slide.

PHOTO/Courtesy Rod Broman

Room 1 of the Grand Rapids German Lutheran School turned out in their best outfits for a class photo in 1886. Elizabeth Bernreuther, right, was their teacher. She was Jane Kitchen's great-grandmother.

PHOTO/Courtesy Jane Kitchen

One of Grand Rapids' friendly establishments welcomed gentlemen to quench dry throats after a long day's labor. A good crowd has already gathered, perhaps for happy hour, as everyone seems to have a fresh pint. There's a handy spittoon, too, ready for service. (Circa 1896).

PHOTO/Courtesy Tim Hunter

This feed store on Market Street was owned by Jetze Van Wetzinga, shown in the front door. You could buy wood, hay, straw and some highly advertised ginger snaps there, too. The photo looks to be from the late 1890s. *PHOTO/Courtesy S.J. King*

Dutch immigrant Jilte Zaagman is shown with his wife, Jennie, in this 1889 photo. Zaagman, a cabinet maker by trade, came to the U.S. in the late 1800s and worked in one of the area's furniture factories before deciding to go into the funeral business. He worked out of the 300 block of Grandville Avenue and, later, from a home at 1033 Sheldon Ave. He purchased 18-inch lumber and made his own caskets. In that day, a coffin cost $5, a grave $2, labor was $2, and a hack (buggy) rented for $3. A license wasn't required in those days, but Mr. Zaagman, in 1902, went to school for three days and obtained license No. 416, one of the first ever issued. Of the couple's two children, William and John, only William went into the family business.

PHOTO/Courtesy Zaagman Family

All right, lads. Look sharp. Mustaches ready. One hundred of the finest officers and patrolmen of the Grand Rapids Police Department were assembled for a photo image in December 1896, taken by T. F. Roble. It appears as though the studio took individual shots of the men and pasted them together to form this noble group. Apparently, the department's tonsorial requirements included a beefy handlebar. A few of the men, new recruits most likely, have yet to come up to standards. Under hat No. 111 (third down in a direct line from hat No. 75 at top, just left of center) is one John Minogue, whose grandson, Tom Chamberlain, has kept the photo all these years.

PHOTO/Courtesy Tom Chamberlain

It was a time when a bow tie could aspire to greatness. These young fellows posing for a photo in 1894 bore them well. That's Edward, left, and John Vandermeer, sons of Jelle and Maggie (Kroodsma) Vandermeer who owned a hardware store on Grandville Avenue and later on Division Avenue. John eventually took over the store. He lived at 29 Holbrook St. in Grand Rapids.

PHOTO/Courtesy Gary and Bette Zandbergen

Julius J. Wagner was a purveyor of groceries and provisions. Originally from Cleveland, Ohio, Wagner lived in Grand Rapids until his death in September 1924. The photo dates from about 1890.

PHOTO/Courtesy John R. Wagner

1900s

Railroad man George A. Lane, far right, and fellow crew members for the Pere Marquette Railroad, take a break from working on rails near the outskirts of Grand Rapids in 1904. He is the grandfather of Tina Lane, who lent this photo. *PHOTO/Courtesy Tina Lane*

Not sure who is who, but Carrie, George and Henry Dice were herded together for a photo (circa 1900) on the northwest side of Grand Rapids. Perhaps the young man has heard stirrings of war news from the Phillipines following the Spanish American War.

PHOTO/Courtesy Karen Hewartson

Nora Husted Carr was a remarkable woman for her time. Divorced in 1885, she came to Grand Rapids and made soap and perfume at home to sell door-to-door to support her five children. She married James C. Carr in the late 1880s and, when he died in 1892, she determined to make her toiletry business something bigger. At a time when women just didn't go into business, she succeeded, founding the Marietta-Stanley Company to market and sell her product, called Sempre Giovine (Italian for forever young). By 1904, she employed 70 people, including her two daughters, Nora and Elizabeth, and a son, Otto. The company continued to thrive under her leadership. When she died in 1915, her daughter, Nora, took the helm. When Nora died in 1935, Elizabeth took charge. The company was closed in 1951 when Elizabeth died and it was sold to Consolidated Chemical of Chicago.

PHOTO/Courtesy Dave Husted

It was either 1903 or 1905 (the chalk character on the slateboard is hard to discern) when this group of children met at Crosby Street School for a photo. It's not known why they are assembled, as school usually ended around mid-June and the little sign says "July 23." Some of those young faces are priceless, apparently chafing at having to dress up and sit still. One of them, Peter Voshel, in the back row, sported a large white bow for the occasion. Probably his mom made him wear it. *PHOTO/Courtesy Ellen Boothe*

Downtown Grand Rapids suffered a terrific flood in 1904. Just months earlier, this was the icy scene at the Pearl Street Bridge.

PHOTO/Courtesy Carole VandenBerg

The School Furniture Co. fielded a hardy team in the early 1900s as the national pastime began to take hold. Three brothers of the Postmus family are among the team members: Andrew, second from left on the bench; Samuel, standing; and John, far right. In 1906, School Furniture became the American Seating Company.

PHOTO/Courtesy Arthur Postmus

Lillian A. White as she appeared in a 1908 portrait. In 1922, after losing her husband several years earlier, Lillian was raising a daughter and living with her father at 30 Lexington Ave. SW, when her dress caught fire while she attempted to light a cookstove. She died from severe burns. She had been employed at Herpolsheimer's and was an expert needleworker.

PHOTO/Courtesy Andrea Edwards

It was a beautiful day in 1909 and Hannah Cromwell may have encouraged her husband, Otto, to take the family to the park. They are photographed on a bench in Campau Park with children, H. William, left, and Frank. Otto was a head blacksmith for the Grand Rapids and Indiana Railroad at the Wyoming yards. Both sons became pharmacists. Frank did well for himself, founding a generic drug company and becoming a millionaire.

PHOTO/Courtesy Mike Cromwell

George Scofield was a widower with two teenage daughters when he came to Grand Rapids around 1900. Realizing that the automobile was an up-and-comer, Mr. Scofield decided to open a "carriage trimming" business on the corner of Front Avenue and Fourth Street NW. He did various work on these new machines, including repairs to the fabric car tops. He is second from right in the photo. His brother, Frank, owned a similar business in Ovid, Mich. Born in April 1853, Mr. Scofield died in April 1940.

PHOTO/Courtesy Joanne Wood

St. Andrews Cathedral is shown in 1903, shortly after a fire caused considerable damage. The structure was built in 1875.

PHOTO/Courtesy Charles Foote

Fresh milk and cream, right to your door. Richard Dykstra and his daughter, Tille, have pure dairy products for sale in this circa 1905 photo. The photo was taken on the west side of Grand Rapids. Tille is the mother of Eleanor Brummel.

PHOTO/Courtesy Eleanor Brummel

Porter Tool & Die was on the northwest side of Grand Rapids in the early 1900s. Alvin H. Porter, cousin of the owner, center in front, is shown in the shop with his co-workers.

PHOTO/Courtesy Barbara J. Guenther

Aunt Mable Mains Olds...

To visit John Ball Park in 1904, you would encounter this entrance, though maybe not the two men. Herman Holmberg is on the right. If you were thirsty, there was a tin cup at the entrance and a supply of water. Just the one tin cup, it is said. Maybe Herman brought his own.

PHOTO/Courtesy Carole VandenBerg

Mable Mains Olds owned a millinery shop in Grand Rapids. Born in 1889 in Toronto, she was described by friends and family as "perky, glamorous, well-dressed and a spit-fire." After retirement, Mable purchased and operated a resort in Grand Haven. She died in 1944. (Photo, circa 1900.)

PHOTO/Courtesy S.J. King

1908

One of the finest conveyances of the day, the No. 346 Lafayette/Stocking streetcar was a sturdy, reliable ride for the urban commuter. Motorman Daniel McSorley, left, was a good man, too. After five years of service, the Grand Rapids Railway Co. presented him a certificate for a "Twenty Dollar Uniform Suit."
PHOTO/Courtesy Judi (Peterson) McSorley

A three-horse-hitch is prepared to launch into action in this 1904 scene. The fire department men were photographed in March 1904, shortly before the great flood of that year. *PHOTO/Courtesy Carole VandenBerg*

1900s

It's fish for dinner, boys. These tough-looking hombres are part of Troop M, 14th U.S. Calvary, out of Fort Grant, Arizona. The lads are photographed somewhere in the Phillipines about 1902-03, a few years after the United States acquired the territory as a result of the short-lived Spanish-American War. Saddler Alfred F. Niggle of Grand Rapids is standing, far right, with a string-full of dinner, er, fish.

PHOTO/Courtesy Carole McKernan

One of Grand Rapids' finest, John Handlogten served briefly on the force from 1908-09. Grandfather of Esther Huizenga, Handlogten was born in Allegan City in 1880 and died Aug. 12, 1961 in Grand Rapids. He lived at 635 Charles St. and is buried in the Garfield Park Cemetery.

PHOTO/Courtesy Esther Huizenga

John and Catherine Schoenhofen pose with their children, Jack and Bob, at 716 Kellogg St. in 1920.

PHOTO/Courtesy Bernard Schoenhofen

A marvelous display of the milliner's craft is offered by these young ladies of 1908. Jan Kitchen's grandmother, Edna Bernreuther is at far left. Splendid job, ladies.

PHOTO/Courtesy Jane Kitchen

George Earl Scofield was a widower with two teenage daughters when he came to Grand Rapids around 1900. Realizing that the automobile was an up-and-comer, Mr. Scofield decided to open a "carriage trimming" business on the corner of Front Avenue and Fourth Street NW. He did various work on these new machines, including repairs to the fabric car tops. He is shown here with two of his customers' cars.

PHOTO/Courtesy Joanne Wood

There was something of a flood in 1904, which this team of fire department horses was negotiating. Looks to have been quite a ride. The scene was near 154 W. Bridge St.

PHOTO/Courtesy Carole VandenBerg

Future business leaders and captains of commerce are shown with the faculty of Grand Rapids Business University, forerunner of Davenport University, in 1901. John M. Bek, front and center between the two older gentlemen, went on to successful careers with Robert W. Irwin Co. and Keeler Brass. According to a history of the city, the first location of the school was in the Luce block, afterward it was in the Ledyard block.

PHOTO/Courtesy Deb Moore

Children of the Evangelical Lutheran School on the West Side of Grand Rapids pose with their teacher, E.H. Dress, who must have had his hands full if this is one class. There are about 70 children pictured here, give or take a couple.

PHOTO/Courtesy Blythe Shirey

"...where everybody knows your name." The friendly neighborhood pub in this photo is Boos Tavern on Alpine Avenue at Richmond Street. Proprietor Frank Boos is on the right in this 1909 photo.

PHOTO/Courtesy Simon Family

Now here was a group of young ladies ready to lighten your day with a musical number. This was the Musical Group of the Swedish Covenant Church, about 1900. Back row from left: Mary Nelson, Hulda Peterson and Ida Wallin. Seated from left: Ellen Berquist, Emma Segarquist, Hulda Lundgren, Lena Ahlberg and Lydia Aspergren.

PHOTO/Courtesy Judi (Peterson) McSorley

The Spruit family is shown in a photo taken in 1906 for relatives in the Netherlands. Jacob, left, John and Peter are in the back. Johanna, John's wife, and the men's father, Nickolas, are in front. The three young men immigrated to the U.S. in the early 1900s to begin a new life. In 1921, they began a coal and building material business at 604 Crosby St. NW. They made their own cement blocks, which bore a trademark that resembled a shoe print. Many homes built on the west side of Grand Rapids used materials from the company. Spruit Bros. is still in business at 550 Richmond St.

PHOTO/Courtesy Schafer Family

Simon Klyn was a musician who immigrated from the Netherlands at age 19. He is shown wearing the uniform of a musical company he joined.

PHOTO/Courtesy Marilyn Klyn Galer

1910s

Boy Scout Troop No. 11 shows its spirit in this 1919 photo. Howard James Foote, 13, fourth from right in the front, was among the best. He was the only scout in the city to receive a medal for selling 10 bonds during the Fifth Victory Loan drive. But then he was just following up, for he also won a medal for the same initiative during the third and fourth loan drives, too.

PHOTO/Courtesy Cynthia (Foote) Osenieks

It was a thriving business in the day. Ice cut from the Grand River would be stored in cool warehouses and sold throughout the city for ice boxes in the kitchen. One of the delivery men was Louis Zandbergen, shown with the reins in his hands in this photo, circa 1910. Louis and his brother, Henry, worked the Wyoming/Grandville area. Lane, the man in the back, is holding a block of ice.

PHOTO/Courtesy Gary and Bette Zandbergen

Grand Rapids Fire Chief Fred Higgins is shown on the right sometime in the 1910s. Chief Higgins did not drive, so always had a driver for his car.

PHOTO/Courtesy Donna Van Dusen

Garrett Idema was all prepared to serve his country during World War I. He was a great cook and the men would have gotten some hardy meals out of him, but he only made it as far as Battle Creek, before the war ended. Oh well.

PHOTO/Courtesy Lou Van Dam

Bert Boerema Sr. and son, Charles, are shown in front of the family home at 1104 Bates St. SE. Bert owned Boerema's Men's Store and was always shown in family photos to be a dapper dresser. The family also loved cars, a trait that was seen early in young Charles.

PHOTO/Courtesy Trudy Boerema Fetters

A dashing George Glupker strikes a pose for a photographer in 1910. The young man would later serve his country in World War I and, while overseas, become stricken by the Spanish Flu (influenza) pandemic of 1918-19. He was sent home to recover. He would later marry, have three children and work in the shipping department for a local cabinet maker.

PHOTO/Courtesy Maureen Walthorn

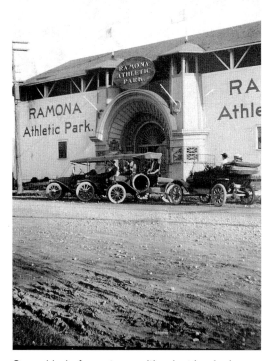

Some kind of event was either just beginning or long over outside the Ramona Athletic Park in East Grand Rapids in the mid to late 1910s.

PHOTO/Courtesy James R. Winslow

It would be hard to find a happier group of guys than these men of the Red Arrow Division returning from World War I and parading in downtown Grand Rapids on May 29, 1919. Front and center is William R. Smith who served in France and Germany and received the French Croix de Guerre with bronze star for "brave and courageous" duty "under a violent fire." Among the many battles in which he fought were the Aisne-Marne Offensive and the Meuse-Argonne Offensive. William married Elizabeth Oakes Smith and had three sons, one who died as an infant, two who served in World War II and one of these in the Korean War. The oldest son, Bill, had a son who would be killed in the Vietnam war. William himself died in 1932 at age 37 from tetanus as the result of an accident at the family cottage near Baldwin, Mich.

PHOTO/Courtesy Sister Michael Ellen Carling

Here's Abe Boerema in 1913, an ambitious and enterprising fellow who began in business by driving for the Baxter Laundry Company. Abe's skills, however, soon had the eye of the Keeler Brass folk and he eventually became an international salesman for that company, traveling throughout the world. He would also join the company's board of directors. Abe and his wife, Grace, had a daughter, Neva, and made their home near Fuller Avenue and Bates Street. The homes in the photo face Bates Street.

PHOTO/Courtesy Christine Boerema Brown

Christian Schroeder was a young man with seafaring dreams when he joined the Navy in 1913. He was assigned to the USS Cummings, a 1,010-ton vessel, for service in Europe.

PHOTO/Courtesy Dolores Schroeder

Cornelius Kamhout, a former Confederate soldier during the War Between the States, is shown in 1914 with 2-year-old Dorothy Blish. Mr. Kamhout lived at the Michigan Veterans Facility. Information with the photo states he served in the 25th Michigan Infantry.

PHOTO/Courtesy M. Maurice Blish

You want a tough crew for iron workers, and these fellows look like they live up to the billing. These guys, including Al Simon, front row at far left, worked at Leitelt Iron Works in 1912.

PHOTO/Courtesy Mary Maksymowski

Police Officer George Ford poses with a motorcycle in front of a house on Kensington Street. (Circa 1919).

PHOTO/Courtesy JoEllen Ford Nickles

The Central High School track team of 1916 was pretty fleet of foot, to judge from those trophies. Among them were Lyman Bacon, top left, and Wendell P. Bacon, bottom row second from left.

PHOTO/Courtesy Barbara Bacon

"I'll give you the moon." At the very least, Arden Fintch and his new bride, Florence (Harden) had a wedding photo taken with the moon at the Ramona Park at Reeds Lake in 1913. Arden later built the "Bow Tie Band" restaurant on Alpine Avenue that was later called the Blue Inn. He was something of a vaudevillian who also operated a small circus and led an orchestra. The couple had one child, a daughter, Donna.

PHOTO/Courtesy Ron Strauss

Mae Dinger and Jack Pfeffer chose the rapids on the Grand River as a spot for this wedding photo in 1910.

PHOTO/Courtesy Simon Family

Sometime in 1918, the U.S. military showcased some of its hardware at a public display set up near Reeds Lake. Minne Boerema and her brother, Charles, posed in front of this giant steam contraption, whose function is not known. The fellows in uniform to the right probably knew.

PHOTO/Courtesy Trudy Boerema Fetters

The Grand Rapids Airplane Co. did its bit for the World War I effort in 1918. They turned out wooden airplane propellers by the dozens. Here, men check a finished propeller inside the Phoenix Furniture Factory.

PHOTO/Courtesy Grand Rapids Public Library

Jim Sloane Sr., left, and buddy pose in doughboy uniforms at the wheel of a sporty car in 1915.

PHOTO/Courtesy Kathy Sloane Wortman

Harold and Ken Vogel are ready to go on an "Irish Mail" in 1918. This interesting vehicle and its kin, are said to have evolved from the velocipedes used by railroad inspectors who rode slowly and close to the track to check out the rails for problems. The company that made them went out of business during the Great Depression.

PHOTO/Courtesy Jane Kitchen

Glenn and Jim Van Otteren ply the waters of the Grand with a craft from the Grand Boat and Canoe Club on North Park Avenue. (Circa 1913).

PHOTO/Courtesy Gordon Van Otteren

One-man performer Arden Fintch is shown with his daughter, Donna, and a variety of instruments in this 1917 photo. The multi-talented Fintch was something of a vaudevillian who also operated a circus in parades on the west side of Grand Rapids and played a massive calliope.

PHOTO/Courtesy Ron Strauss

All you needed to have a good time with your friends in 1913 was a deck of cards and a mom to bring out the occasional snack. This lively group included, from left: Fred Boersma, Rena Boersma, Hermina Holtrop, Jennie Boersma, Alice DeHaan and Henry Holtrop. That's mom and aunt Clara Boersma behind the group.

PHOTO/Courtesy Anna M. Rockwell

W.E. Briggs helped run his family's 80-acre Oak Grove Dairy on what is now Plainfield Avenue. The family settled the homestead in 1850. The Overland car pictured in this 1913 photo had already traveled more than 77,000 miles, according to a newspaper article that covered the unusual feat, noting that milk routes were not confined to smooth pavements. Briggs told the newspaper that he expected the car was "still good for a whole lot of service."
PHOTO/Courtesy Jeanne Briggs

This photo, dating to around the late 1910s, was among the effects of Adolph Kurz who died leaving no relatives. Kurz was a linotype operator for the Grand Rapids Herald and this photo may show him with co-workers in the Herald linotype room around that period. Kurz also served in the Armed Forces during World War I. In 1967, the Doezema family purchased the house in which Kurz lived at 1841 Martin SE with all its contents.

PHOTO/Courtesy Mary Ann Doezema

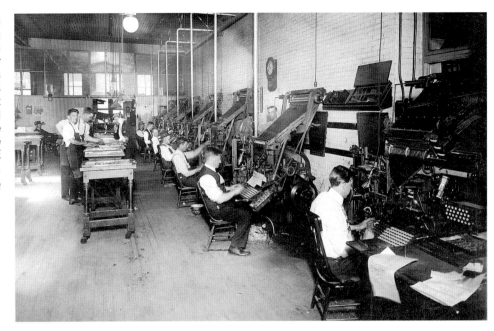

Lena Gmelich poses on Library Street for a photo near Veteran's Park in 1910. The Grand Rapids Herald building is in the background.

PHOTO/Courtesy Eikenhout/Pettinga Families

Young musicians of the St. Alphonsus music group are shown during a break from practice, circa 1917. Loretta Knight, who played piano, is wearing a plaid dress, third from right.

PHOTO/Courtesy Catherine Haney

Golden Jubilee of Ven. Mother Aquinata Gran

From the archives at Marywood comes this photo of Sisters who have gathered to commemorate the golden jubilee of Mother Aquinata Fiegler at St. John's Home in Grand Rapids on Aug. 4, 1914. The Sisters worked in parish schools in the Diocese of Grand Rapids. St. John's Home was the Motherhouse of the Dominican Sisters until they moved to the Marywood facility off Fulton Street NE in 1922.

PHOTO/Courtesy Sister Michael Ellen Carling

Aug. 4. 1914

Young men and women of 1916 learn the intricacies of the minuet at dance class.

PHOTO/Courtesy Kathy Sloane Wortman

The men of the No. 2 Firehouse on Barclay Street. Driving the team is Byron Lewis who worked as a fireman from 1909-1915 and as a police officer from the 1920s-1940s. He was a logger in between. Lewis said he preferred police work.

PHOTO/Courtesy Lisa Lewis Koster

Though it was not Cuba, you could still find a fine cigar in the early days of Grand Rapids, especially if you ordered from the William Callaghan Cigar Co. on Michigan Street near Monroe Avenue. This 1913 photo shows the interior of the store. Louis Callaghan, son of the owner, is seated second from left. A bin of tobacco leaves is at right where a woman sits before a rolling board.

PHOTO/Courtesy Helen Foley

In 1917, Charles Van Valkenburg made a living transporting luggage for arriving passengers at the Plainfield Avenue and Leonard Street train station. He's shown with his truck, a very sturdy looking REO Speed Wagon. The photo was taken at 340 Spencer St. (REO, by the way, were the initials for Ransom E. Olds, who made the vehicles and later founded the Oldsmobile brand.)

PHOTO/Courtesy Cynthia L. Morren

It was 1917 and the country was at war. Strict lights-out policies were observed at night, a fact that would cause trouble for 7-year-old Charlie Boerema. He and three of his family were returning from a church outing one evening – no headlights allowed – when their car was hit by a train. "It was like hitting a tuna fish can," he later recalled to family, "that car just blew apart." But, no one was seriously injured. Charlie, in this photo, is looking very much a wounded veteran in uniform, but in fact is sporting a bandage as a result of a scrape he suffered in that accident.

PHOTO/Courtesy Trudy Boerema Fetters

Apple picking time in 1908. Albert and Elizabeth Rohloff packed up the kids and made a day of it at their homestead on Cogswell Street NW. The kids include Dorothy, Anthony, Carl, Albert, Edward, Henry, Gertrude and John. Dad must be pointing out where some of the prime apples are waiting.

PHOTO/Courtesy Roger Rohloff

Dressed perhaps for a chilly day, this family got together in 1910 for a bit of an outing in its new Austin automobile. Dad's got on his leather driving gloves and seems to have things well in hand. It's unknown exactly where in Grand Rapids the photo was taken.

PHOTO/Courtesy Grand Rapids Public Library

It was a grand day at a fair in Comstock Park in 1912, with a lot of activity around the S.J. Harden candy stand. Kids are waiting for pulled taffy. There's even a fellow on crutches, perhaps a Spanish American War veteran. Samuel J. Harden, with the mustache and cap, is overseeing things while his wife, Emma, is at the taffy hook.

PHOTO/Courtesy Ron Strauss

Ramona Park of East Grand Rapids was quite the destination in its heyday with lots of entertainment and activities, including having a photo taken with your friends. Here, Mary Rejent, left, poses with a couple of pals.

PHOTO/Courtesy Mary Jane Woods

Ahh, young love. It was early in 1914 and all the world lay at their feet. Ray Thomas Goss and Sylvia Spoelstra would marry and rear nine children. The family lived on Shamrock Street, east of Grandville Avenue.

PHOTO/Courtesy Jon and Lynn Goss

The Wurzburgs team could not be beat on the lanes in 1917. Among them was Al Simon, second from right, a tool & die maker at Leitelt Iron Works.

PHOTO/Courtesy Mary Maksymowski

1910s

Stickley. There's a name that means something to those who know fine furniture. This view shows the rear of the Stickley Brothers Company factory about 1918. It was located at 837-861 Godfrey Ave. SW. Known for its Arts and Crafts style, Stickley operated from 1891 until 1954.

PHOTO/Courtesy Grand Rapids Public Library

A wedding day photograph? Catherine Haney thinks so. This is a photo of her aunts taken on Aug. 31, 1913. Catherine believes it was the wedding day of Mary Knight, left, shown with her sisters, Anna, middle, and Helena. Mary became Mary Kline. The young women are dressed stylishly with long-sleeve dresses, broad hats, white gloves and purses. The photo may have been taken along the Grand River or perhaps at Reeds Lake.

PHOTO/Courtesy Catherine Haney

Charles Clayton Booth and his two sturdy equine friends delivered coal for the A.B. Knowlson Co. The company was located about where the present Amtrak station is on Market Street and Wealthy Avenue. The photo was taken on July 4, 1919.

PHOTO/Courtesy Booth Family

The Nauta clan is pictured in front of their store on Kalamazoo Avenue and Adams Street sometime between 1910 and 1920. Dirck and Alice Nauta ran the store. Among other things, it sold tobacco (Duke's Mixture), Red Crown gasoline, was a steam laundry and a post office.

PHOTO/Courtesy Gordon Nauta

When folks needed goods, they headed to the E.J. Norden General Store at 581 Leonard St. NW, which offered just about anything you would need. Ebel John Norden at the rear is shown with his children, Dena, John, Etta and Henrietta. His wife, Wibbiena, is holding Dick. This store is just chock full of good things.

*PHOTO/Courtesy
Don Morren Family*

Around 1917, Frank and Jessie Chrystler lived at 616 Bates St. SE, as did all the little Chrystlers, seven of them. Back, from left: Jessie, Harold, Dora and Nellie. Front, from left: Hazel, George, Edith, Frank and Mildred, who got caught laughing at Nellie. Frank was an engineer for the Grand Rapids Fire Department, Engine Co. No. 6 at Ellsworth and Grandville Avenue. He served with the company from 1914 to 1943.

*PHOTO/Courtesy
Sherry VanOeveren Bouwman*

Harry Brummel, left, and his brother, Fred, pose outside Harry's barber shop on Cherry Street in 1913.

PHOTO/Courtesy Harry Brummel

Bernadine Reynolds poses with a milk wagon belonging to her father, Michael. Pure Jersey milk and cream was available from Madison Square Dairy in 1914.

PHOTO/Courtesy Deb Moore

A grand day out for the young folk. Patrice Kuiper and Albert Rodenhouse were in the back seat. Albert's brother, Nicholas, was driving and Johannah Vanderveen was his front-seat partner during a Memorial Day celebration in 1914. Nicholas would later become a skilled bookbinder, one of the last in Grand Rapids at his retirement in 1951.

PHOTO/Courtesy Marian Grant

1920s

The mighty Ajax football (soccer) team played at John Ball Park on Sunday afternoons. The men were all immigrants. A few names in this 1925 photo are known. Arie Shellenberg is at far left. Arie DePuy is the fellow in black and Louis Battstra is to his right. Wynand DePuy is kneeling, second from left.

PHOTO/Courtesy J. Machielse

It was a grand day whenever the Benevolent and Protective Order of Elks decided a parade was in order. In this circa 1920 photo, the BPOE were in full regalia for a march through downtown Grand Rapids. It was a gala time for all.

*PHOTO/Courtesy
Grand Rapids Public Library*

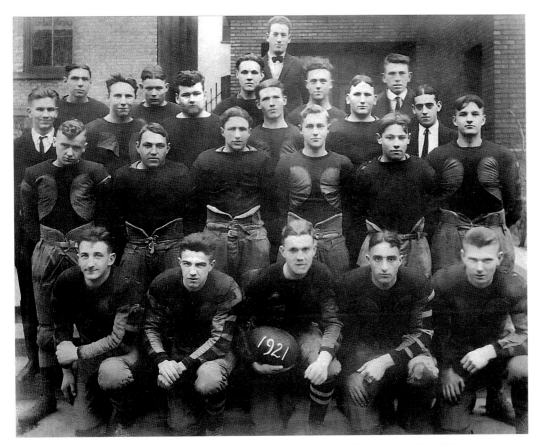

It was a tough group of lads who turned out for football at Union High School in 1921.
John Weidenfeller is in the back row, fifth from left.

PHOTO/Courtesy Marlene Fabbro

Playmates Marvin Weemhof and Anna Mae
Holtrop seem ready from some winter fun in
1927 in a sled with a Teaberry Gum box seat.
The photo was taken at 919 Baxter St. SE.

PHOTO/Courtesy Anna M. Rockwell

It wasn't a sleep-over. Young lady athletes of the 1920s wore such attire when they competed in various events. Here, a group of smiling athletes of Widdicomb School are shown with a trophy they won at a city track and field competition. Marian DeHamer, (middle row, second from left) was one member of the victorious team.

PHOTO/Courtesy Ellen Boothe

Now that's a pedal car, er, plane. Jack Rocks is the happy pilot, pictured in front of his house in 1925, at 425 Graham St. NW.

PHOTO/Courtesy Kathy Scheer

Frank Bacon, an educator for 52 years, taught at Central High School and was the chief organizer of citizenship classes. His granddaughter, Barbara Bacon, said that he "always felt that the most priceless gift to the people who live in this country is their citizenship." (Circa 1920).

PHOTO/Courtesy Barbara Bacon

Get out and vote, good citizens – that was the message for a primary election in September 1924 from the Grand Rapids League of Women Voters. David and Mary Amberg are next to their mom, Mrs. Julius H. Amberg. Also urging citizens to vote are Florence Shelley and Grace Van Hoesen. And vote early, by the way.

PHOTO/Courtesy Grand Rapids Public Library

CHAMPIONS - 1929

Football (soccer) men of 1929, and champions, too, but it is not known of what league. Named the Independence, the team was said to have played prison teams among their other challengers. Hank Wehrman is second from right at top. The team was started by Joseph Egner and Wynand DePuy.

PHOTO/Courtesy J. Machielse

A young man and his flying machine. Glenn Van Otteren, 21, poses in 1928 with the club plane of the Grand Rapids Flying Club, formerly the Aero Club and soon to be the Kent Flying Club. Glenn had four siblings and they all, including their parents, had private pilot licenses.

PHOTO/Courtesy Gordon Van Otteren

In a photo estimated to be from about 1921, Joe DeBoer is at the wheel of a "dragster" style car that he built. Looks like a pretty mean machine.

PHOTO/Courtesy S.J. King

Here's some fellows up to no good. Actually, it's the Grand Rapids Fire Department baseball team of 1920 having a little fun. John Koepke, front right, worked in the department for 25 years. *PHOTO/Courtesy Katherine Dykstra*

This bulky steam contraption was used on the Briggs Homestead (shown in the photo below), an 80-acre dairy farm that was among the oldest of settled areas in Kent County. It was begun by a New York state couple who moved to Ann Arbor in 1834 before settling in the wilds of Kent County in 1850. The house still stands at Plainfied and Arlington Street NE and is the third oldest home in the city. The site was declared a historic landmark by the city in 1979 and later placed on the state Register of Historic Sites. About 11 acres of the farm were turned into a children's park and city pool that still carries the Briggs name.

PHOTO/Courtesy Jeanne Briggs

This photo could have been lifted from one of the "Our Gang" comedies of the 1930s. But that's Peter Compaan and his buddies on Kalamazoo Avenue about 1925. Peter's the one in the front on the left.

PHOTO/Courtesy Carole Compaan Mieras

Little Shirley Smith and her brother, Freddy, are well bundled against the spring air in April 1926 outside their home at 545 Worden SE. Freddy would fall victim to measles in 1935 at 13 years old.

PHOTO/Courtesy Janice Snyder

A pony picture for 1924. Joseph Skok got the saddle. That's Julia with the cat and Louie who is looking on.

PHOTO/Courtesy Norma Corby

The Furniture City Upholstery Co. had its first plant in this building on S. Division Avenue. The company later moved to a place on Butterworth Avenue and Front Street on the Grand River. (Circa 1920).

PHOTO/Courtesy Gordon Van Otteren

The A.B. Knowlson Co. did not fare so well from a tornado that struck the area sometime in 1924. Harry Booth was put in charge of the cleanup, which must have been a considerable job. The site was located about where the current Amtrak station is on Market Street and Wealthy Avenue.

PHOTO/Courtesy Booth Family

In the days before flight delays and lost luggage, Stout Airlines was the first strictly passenger airline in the nation, with a route between Grand Rapids and Detroit. This 1927 photo shows one of the craft. One way was $16, round trip was $32.

PHOTO/Courtesy Eikenhout/Pettinga Families

A 1923 music ensemble from Catholic Central High School included the unusual addition of the drummer. Most chamber ensembles were of strings or the occasional piano and wind instrument. But it was a lucky addition for Catherine Haney as her parents, George Haney (the drummer) and Loretta Knight, the pianist, met through this group.

PHOTO/Courtesy Catherine Haney

Pfc. John P. Koepke is home safe from World War I in this early 1920s photo. With him is his mother, Mary Catherine Czerwinski Koepke. John served with the 339 Infantry, Polar Bear Division, in Russia. He later became a fireman, serving for 25 years in the Grand Rapids Fire Department.

PHOTO/Courtesy Katherine Dykstra

Industrious scouts are busy at a log cabin project near Burlingame Avenue in this 1920s photo. Maury Blish is in the middle on top. At far right, Cameron Bell directs the activity.

PHOTO/Courtesy M. Maurice Blish

Immigrants were arriving in record numbers during the first decades of the 20th Century. Many found homes and employment in the Grand Rapids-area furniture industry. To help the newest members of the USA, the American Seating Co. held Americanization Classes for its workers, taught by instructors from YMCA Industrial Services. This photo from around 1920 shows such a class, with the guys all ready to learn about the American way.

PHOTO/Courtesy Grand Rapids Public Library

Just off a winning season, the Johnson-Handley-Jonhson Furniture Co. team posed for the camera. Team catcher William DeBruyn, second from left, and his brother James, fourth from left, were on the 1927 softball team. William worked for Johnson-Handley-Johnson as well as Berkey & Gay. He and his wife, Luella, lived in Grand Rapids.

PHOTO/Courtesy Family of Stewart and Barbara Miller

The lads of the 2nd Regiment have a long and storied history. In 1855, the Grand Rapids Light Guard and Grand Rapids Artillery companies were organized and in 1859, the Grand Rapids Rifles came into existence. These companies joined with others to form the 51st Volunteer Uniformed Michigan Militia Regiment. These formed the core of the Third Michigan, which fought 12 campaigns during the Civil War. In 1874, the Grand Rapids Guard became Company B 2nd Infantry Regiment. The 2nd later was redesignated the 32nd Volunteer Infantry Regiment for duty in the Spanish-American War and, in 1916, for duty along the Mexican border. The 32nd was later activated for World War I as part of the 32nd Division. Under command of Colonel Joseph Westnedge, the 32nd became the 126th Infantry Regiment, served with distinction in France and earned the French Croix de Guerre, but lost its dearly beloved Colonel Westnedge to the effects of mustard gas. It has since been known as the 126th Infantry Regiment and most lately as the 1-126 Calvary and has seen distinguished duty in other combat theaters. The photo of the band likely dates from the late teens or early '20s.

PHOTO/Courtesy Joyce Collins

Meats and groceries could be found at The Great Atlantic & Pacific Tea Co. store at 746 S. Division Ave. This scene is circa 1925. Looks like there's some good produce outside, too.

PHOTO/Courtesy Ed Paciencia

The summer after they graduated from Catholic Central High School (1925), George "Fran" Haney, right, and his best friend, Louis Orth, took off for a cross-country tour in a vehicle they built. Those were the days, eh. Check out the glasses. One hopes the lads didn't encounter any nasty storms.

PHOTO/Courtesy Catherine Haney

Sometime in the 1920s, a Harrison Park Elementary class escaped its confines to set up camp in Harrison Park. The young men are engaged in a war dance, it seems, perhaps on the lookout for school authorities, while the young women are beating a cadence with their hands and a gourd.

PHOTO/Courtesy Karen Hewartson

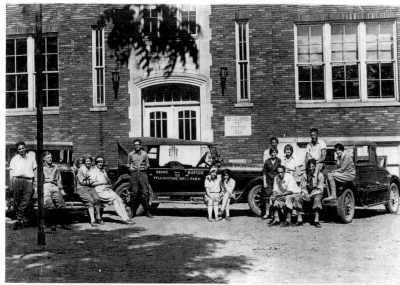

Getting ready for a big class trip to Yellowstone National Park is the 1929 graduating class of Godwin High School. It will be quite a trip in those old roadsters, but this hardy crew looks like they can't wait.

PHOTO/Courtesy Ron Strauss

Shorty Fisher, left, and Raymond Rafferty were a couple of dapper mail carriers in the late teens and early 1920s. Here, they posed by a friend's car.

PHOTO/Courtesy Richard Rafferty

Simon Klyn, a musician, immigrated from the Netherlands in 1902 at age 19. He established himself in Grand Rapids, formed a band, married and reared nine children with his wife, Jennie. You'll find him in front of the drum at lower right with one of his children. His band had been hired to play at the annual picnic of the Leonard Refrigerator Co. in 1924.

PHOTO/Courtesy Marilyn Klyn Galer

In June 1927, aspiring thespians of Grand Rapids Junior College staged "The Enemy." Seven-year-old Lucille Mae Cunningham, center, played a young boy and was one of the students at Margaret Fealy's "The Fealy School of Dramatic Expression." She could later say that she trod the boards with the likes of Spencer Tracy, Dean Jager and Selina Royale.

PHOTO/Courtesy James R. Winslow

In the spring of 1927, a few ladies went off for a bit of fresh air. Jo Wendler is standing, Dorothy Wendler is sitting on the running board and Margaret Oakes, mother of Sister Michael Ellen Carling, is inside the car. No word on who the woman is who had to sit out in the rumble seat. But she looks well bundled against the chill.

PHOTO/Courtesy Sister Michael Ellen Carling

Chances are that calendar on your wall from the mid-1920s came from this fine shop at 906-912 S. Division Ave. And if the company's employees felt like a bit of snacking, well, the Grand Rapids Potato Chip Co. was right downstairs.

PHOTO/Courtesy Ed Paciencia

William Zaagman, son of Jilte Zaagman, who founded the Zaagman Memorial Chapel in 1890, is shown in 1926 with the company's hearse, a coach built by Sayers & Scovill of Cincinnati, Ohio. The photo was taken near Bates Street and Eastern Avenue. William's only other sibling, John, went into business in California.

PHOTO/Courtesy Zaagman Family

Three-year-old Ed Cwiklinski seems to have already established a solid work ethic in this 1924 photo. He would later work for American Seating and eventually marry a co-worker, Eleanor Duba. The couple did not marry until their early '50s and would remain married for the next 33 years. Ed passed away on Dec. 22, 2004. Eleanor followed three years later to the day.

PHOTO/Courtesy Maureen Walthorn

In 1928, the Square Deal Restaurant was a favorite lunch spot for Sligh Furniture Co. workers who were just a block away and rushed to the eatery when the noon whistle blew. But all was lost next year when the stock market crashed and Peter John Lybaart, center behind the counter, had to sell. To his right is his wife, Martha, and on his left, his daughter, Lorene. The fellow at the far left is counterman, Billie Calhoun.

PHOTO/Courtesy Maxine Lybaart Zeigler

Former members of the American North Russia Expeditionary Force, nicknamed the Polar Bears, are shown making a stop in Grand Rapids in the winter of 1927. The 339th U.S. Infantry, composed of Michigan soldiers, fought a huge battle against Russian forces near Archangel, Russia, on Nov. 11 1918, while the rest of the world was celebrating the armistice agreement that ended World War I.

PHOTO/Courtesy Grand Rapids Public Library

The young gridiron warriors of South High School posed for this portrait in 1941. The guys went on to post a winning record of 4-0-2 for the season. Coach Al Vanderbush later coached at Hope College. Robert "Rip" Collins, No. 41 in the back row, also played at Hope College and coached at Ottawa Hills High School. Rip was the first coach for the fledgling football program at Grand Valley State University in 1971 and '72, although his teams failed to post a single win.

PHOTO/Courtesy Joyce Collins

Just married and on the cusp of the Great Depression, John A. Van Houten and his bride, Jacoba (Kremers) sat for a photo on their wedding day – May 23, 1929. Jacoba, a German immigrant, and John would have five children. He worked as a male nurse at Pine Rest, had an ash pickup route and later found employment at the General Motors plant on 36th Street, from which he retired. Jacoba worked at Stickley Brothers furniture for a time, but devoted herself to raising those five children.

PHOTO/Courtesy Gerry Buurstra

A Grand Rapids Herald delivery van and driver were photographed in a local neighborhood in this 1920 photograph.

PHOTO/Courtesy Grand Rapids Public Library

John Rocks, right, and a friend are shown outside a bicycle repair shop on Grandville Avenue in this scene that dates from some time in the 1920s.

PHOTO/Courtesy Kathy Scheer

Put that camera down, now! Ira Stout of the Grand Rapids Police Department shows would-be felons that he is a man of stern material. (Circa 1920).

PHOTO/Courtesy Bob Duell

Young men, and a few ladies, are bent to the task of learning the fine art of furniture design at Davis Tech, under the tutelage of Herman Holmberg, standing at center in the white smock. At top left, facing the room, is his son, Arthur. (Circa 1925).

PHOTO/Courtesy Carole VandenBerg

For hire. Lyman Flynn was in his mid-20s, had a motorcar and was ready at a moment's notice to take you where you wanted to go in Grand Rapids. The cabby poses with his car in this 1923 photo.

PHOTO/Courtesy Margaret Kimber

Kids just can't help but smile when they get on a pony. So it was with Robert and Katherine Booth when their opportunity came up in 1929, thanks to a local farmer who brought a pony to the neighborhood. The photo was taken on Cole Avenue.

PHOTO/Courtesy Booth Family

This circa 1920s photo from the Wyoming Historical Commission shows a few of the local lads near the Silver Foam Saloon on Godfrey Avenue and Chicago Drive. Occasionally, it is said, the area's Dutch farmers would stop for a refreshing beverage while transporting goods to market.

PHOTO/Courtesy Ron Strauss

1930s

This 1931 photo shows a ladder truck and its proud operators. John P. Koepke, who operated the truck's rear steering, is second from left.
PHOTO/Courtesy Katherine Dykstra

John's Confectionery Shop, 1151 S Division Ave., was a nice place to while away a happy hour or two. There were a variety of candies and soda shop specialties, including select cigars. For a nickel, you could get a tune out of a player piano, too. John Geluso, second from right, and his wife Rose, reared six children. In 1939-40, the shop was leased to become Pete's Hamburger and Rib Shop.

PHOTO/Courtesy Anne (Geluso) Valentine

The 11 children of the Julien family pose with their parents at 1025 Chatham St. SW in this early 1930s photo. The family was instrumental in the founding of St. James Catholic Church. Back row from left: Irene, Irving, Genevieve, William, Lillian, Cora, Ralph and Dorothy. Seated, from left: Harry, George (father), Mary (mother), George W. and Modesta.

PHOTO/Courtesy Carole McKernan

Things WERE bigger in the good old days. Take an ice cream cone for example. Jessie Decker, 4, may not have had this size in mind when she requested a treat. The photo was taken in 1934 on the corner of Marion Avenue and Fulton Street near John Ball Zoo. The giant cone was perched on a stand and was probably an advertisement for a local ice cream shop.

PHOTO/Courtesy Mark Lammers

Claude O. Taylor Sr. and wife, Mabel, pose at the center of a Christmas family gathering. Taylor was a union man, secretary of the Trades Council and held every office in the Barber's Union. He was influential in the Furniture Strike of 1911 and the 1913 Copper Strike in the Upper Peninsula.

PHOTO/Courtesy Jeri Taylor Holzgen

Fighting George Warner had the right stuff to become a Golden Gloves champion. Warner competed in 76 bouts and won more than 50 by knockout. He became the first state champion from Grand Rapids when he won a bantamweight final in 1932. A year earlier he fought in the National Golden Gloves tournament at New York's Madison Square Garden, where he made it to the semifinals. To keep his weight down while in New York, his trainers wrapped him in a rubber suit and had him work out in the hot sun on the roof of their hotel. His daughter, Blythe Shirey, still has all the keepsakes from her father's boxing career.

PHOTO/Courtesy Blythe Shirey

Here's something you don't see every day: an aerial view of Grand Rapids from about 1939. Things have changed a bit. That's the Bridge Street bridge and the west side canal is still in place. Even the Civic Auditorium can be made out just below the airplane wing. The photo, by the way, was taken and developed by amateur photographer Jerry Ehtingh.

*PHOTO/Courtesy
Anna M. Rockwell*

Kenneth C. Lyon played baseball for Union High School in 1938-39. Looks like a young Yogi Berra, the famous catcher for the New York Yankees.

PHOTO/Courtesy Donna Lyon

Mary had a little dog who followed her to school one day. Mary, seated far right, is Mary DeBruyn and the dog is Daisy, who visited the second grade at Harrison Park School in 1930. The kids are practicing drawing, writing and story skills with Daisy as the subject.

PHOTO/Courtesy Mary Nozal

Alice Davey's parents, Bill and Verna Johnell (left and middle), met at a candy store he owned in Muskegon, the Liberty Candy Kitchen. Bill, a Greek immigrant, lost the store during the Great Depression, but did not give up. In this photo from 1938, he and Verna are working at Chris' Hamburg Shop on Division Avenue north of Burton Street. Bill eventually saved enough to open another place, the Blackstone Cafe, at 411 Leonard St. NW.

PHOTO/Courtesy Alice Davey

It was a well-mannered kindergarten class that posed with their teacher in 1935 on the steps of the Fairmount Elementary, 2042 Oakwood Ave. NE. Looks like she ran a pretty tight ship. Well, all except for the one fellow at lower left who was distracted when the photographer snapped the picture. But that didn't bother little Bob Hall, front and center in his snappy tie and buckle shoes.

PHOTO/Courtesy Kenneth Cherry Photography

A group of friends pose in the snow in 1939 outside Seymour Christian School. From left: Margaret Wiersum, Bernice Haveman, Tressa Buikema, Anna Mae Holtrop, Kathryn Mulder and Marian Batts.

PHOTO/Courtesy Anna M. Rockwell

Sworn to uphold the law and keep the peace, the men of the Grand Rapids Police Department, circa 1932, pose for a photo outside headquarters.
PHOTO/Courtesy Shippy Family

Paul Whiteman was a popular local band leader, who conducted various bands. He appears in this 1938 photo with an unknown orchestra at Bigelow Field in Grand Rapids. Whatever was going on, the stands seem packed.

PHOTO/Courtesy
Grand Rapids Public Library

The Great Depression had just kicked in, but Leona VanDyke and her family were holding their own. In fact, Leona had at least $575, which was enough money to buy a new 1931 Chevy Roadster.

PHOTO/Courtesy Cynthia L. Morren

Remember the old steamer at Ramona Park on Reeds Lake? These people likely do. It was a Sunday School outing in the mid-30s and Mavis Ryskamp, left, Marilyn Bomers, Donna Bos, Berdelia Vander Vennen, Elaine Bylsma and Lou Van Dam had a great time on board.

PHOTO/Courtesy Lou Van Dam

Men of the Simon family gather to celebrate the end of Prohition in 1932. The Simon men, all of German descent, knew and appreciated a good beverage. The fellow on the left did a lot of appreciating.

PHOTO/Courtesy Simon Family

Based upon their studies of the Far East, the first grade girls of Oakleigh School dressed up in Japanese kimonos for a picture in 1930.

PHOTO/Courtesy Marian Grant

Cheryl Berman's mom, Jeanette DeMaagd, second from right, and three friends had themselves a day at the movies in 1938. "White Banners" was playing at the Paramount, starring Claude Rains and Fay Bainter.

PHOTO/Courtesy Cheryl Berman

Here's the fourth grade of Fairmount Elementary School on Oakwood Avenue NE in 1934. The teacher apparently has a stern and watchful eye on some poor scholar she suspects of harboring mischievious plans.

PHOTO/Courtesy Noorthoek Family

The team is hitched and the kids are ready for a hay ride in this 1935 photo. The location is somewhere in the greater Grand Rapids area, but the barn and location are not identified. Everybody looks in good spirits for the ride, though.

PHOTO/Courtesy Grand Rapids Public Library

Marguerite Bouwens – middle row, second from left – is shown with her high school basketball team, circa 1935.

PHOTO/Courtesy Charles Bouwens

It's true... there was more snow back in the day. That's the East Beltline (yes, THE East Beltline) somewhere near Knapp Street in February 1936. And that's Jerry Warmolt's car on the one cleared (somewhat) lane. Commuting has changed a bit since then.

PHOTO/Courtesy Mary Douthett

He looked like a tough hombre, but Erwin Sullivan was a great father and a fine foreman at Wolverine Carton Co. where he worked from 1934 to 1970. He poses here with a new 1937 Ford on a December day in 1937.

PHOTO/Courtesy John Sullivan

What we have here is a mystery. Sometime during the late 1930s, Murl Whalley and his Band produced "sweet and suave music" in the Grand Rapids area. But, information about Murl and his band is hard to come by. What we do know is that the sax player immediately to the right of the trumpet player in the foreground (Murl?) was Ray Kuzniak, a local musician. Hard to fathom why Murl and the boys never made it big. How can you beat "sweet and suave?"

PHOTO/Courtesy Stephen Smith

THE SWEET & SUAVE MUSIC OF MURL WHALLEY AND HIS BAND

Times were hard during the Depression. Many found work where they could. A Works Progress Administration (WPA) crew was photographed in May 1934 in the Diamond Street NE area where they were developing the street's intersection at Fulton Avenue. The WPA was a relief measure established in 1935 and headed by Harry L. Hopkins. It offered work to the unemployed by spending money on a wide variety of programs, including highways and building construction, slum clearance, reforestation and rural rehabilitation. The hope was to stimulate private business during the depression years. Peter Faasse, father of the photo's owner, worked for the WPA. The fellow without a shovel and wearing a bow tie to the left of center was likely the crew chief. The photo was taken by Charles Harshberger.

PHOTO/Courtesy Marcus Faasse

Photo By
Chas. I. Harshbarger
May 25 1934

The city of Grand Rapids thought this area would be a great one for its new civic auditorium named after George Welsh, a former mayor. But engineers thought the east bank of the Grand River required a bit of shoring up, so strong men were found to help make the foundation secure in advance of the actual construction work. This photo from August 1931 shows the site as it looked during this time.

PHOTO/Courtesy
Grand Rapids Public Library

Alvin Patterson Sr. was manager of Kroger Dairy in the 1920s and '30s. He was very good at his job and served as a sort of trouble-shooter for dairies around the U.S.

PHOTO/Courtesy Don Meinke

The local paper of the day had a column called "Hum of the Business World." One day, in the early 1930s, it contained this item: "George Scofield has obtained a permit to erect a cement block oil station at 429 Front Ave. NW. The estimated cost is $2,000." He had previously operated an Auto and Carriage Trimming shop on Front Avenue and Fourth Street NW. He is shown here with a new state-of-the-art Sunoco gasoline pump at his new station.

PHOTO/Courtesy Joanne Wood

Meeting to hash things over, get things right and move the congregation in the right direction was the General Synod of the Reformed Church of America. They gathered for their deliberations at the Central Reformed Church, corner of Fountain Street and Barclay Avenue, in June 1934.

PHOTO/Courtesy Central Reformed Church

Sisters Verona, 24, left, and Adorah Curtis, 26, were a handsome pair of young ladies back in 1935. They're pictured in front of their home at 619 Logan St. SE. Verona later married and had one daughter, Sue.

PHOTO/Courtesy Susie E. Curtis

Their chores done, the kids hitched up Molly and went for a wagon ride down Leffingwell Avenue on a fine day in 1935. That's Jay Doezema with the reins, and Marion Mol, left, Lois Mol and Ken Doezema giggling behind him. Jay is actually wearing driving goggles. The Doezema farm was at Leffingwell Avenue and Knapp Street NE, about where the Kent Skills Center is today.

PHOTO/Courtesy Doezema Family

On July 18, 1935, Lester Voshel and Marian DeHamer were married. He was 23 and she was 19. In the photo, the newly married Mrs. Voshel is wearing a lavender dress with a purple bow. Bride and groom were both born and reared on the west side of Grand Rapids. After they were married, they built a home on Covell Road NW, where they reared two children, Ellen and Jerry. Lester was a homebuilder and worked for Werner Machinery during World War II and later retired from that company. Marian looked after the family and was active in Oakleigh School PTA and at Richmond Reformed Church.

PHOTO/Courtesy Ellen Boothe

Parishioners of Our Lady of Sorrows Church gather for a photo
following a Parish Mission in March 1931. The Grand Rapids Italian
Band provided the stirring music for the occasion. The church
celebrated its centennial in 2008. The church is at 101 Hall St. SE.

PHOTO/Courtesy Gasper Amodeo

This scene circa 1930 shows the "Compo Mounting Room" of the Luce Furniture Company. It looks like it was a very busy place.

*PHOTO/Courtesy
Barbara Sue Damore*

A fire department training exercise sometime in the 1930s found one fellow strapped to a stretcher being lowered, while John P. Koepke supervised from the ladder.

*PHOTO/Courtesy
Katherine Dykstra*

Harry Booth thought the idea of an overhead garage door was the bees knees. An enterprising fellow, he started right in and is said to have installed the first such door in Grand Rapids. His father, Charles, worked with him and together they installed 16 such doors at the Interstate Motor Freight Co. They would have kept going, too, had not the supply of steel been curtailed by World War II. The business folded as a result. He is pictured here in 1939.

PHOTO/Courtesy Booth Family

Having failed in their mission to blow up the lab, the South High School chemistry class of 1938 went outside, tubes and bottles in hand, to reconsider their methods. Or at least to have a group picture. All the kids signed the back of this particular photo. Among them, Wes Shusta, Bob Werner, George Ohland, Norma Mitchell (in the plaid jacket) and Peter Mitchell (back row, far right.)

PHOTO/Courtesy Mitchell Family

John Collins Park now occupies the area in this 1935 photograph of Reeds Lake. The little steamer, Ramona, chugs along the shore while sailboats skim the lake in the background. Except for the steamship and the older cars, the scene is not far different from today.

PHOTO/Courtesy Grand Rapids Public Library

D'Amico's Food Market has been a longtime fixture in Grand Rapids, serving up quality food and good service since 1906. Meat was certainly a favorite. The store in this 1936 photo was at 747 S. Division Ave. It is now at 1747 Plainfield Ave. NE and under the fifth generation of family operation. At left is Anna D'Amico. The young fellow behind her is James P. Spica, who is now 82 and still involved in the business. Paul D'Amico is the man in the rear with the apron. Sam D'Amico is in the foreground with an apron. Barely seen to the right, behind the counter, is Rose D'Amico.

PHOTO/Courtesy James P. Spica Sr. Family

Grand Rapids Police Department Patrolman Melvin Shippy also played baseball for the force. Games were held at Ramona Park field circa 1934.

PHOTO/Courtesy Shippy Family

They were tough guys at Creston High School – practicing with helmets was for the weaker fellows of other schools. "Lugging the Mail" here is Joseph "Joey" Noorthoek, at far left during a practice in 1939. He was named to the All City and All State teams.

PHOTO/Courtesy Noorthoek Family

Byron William Lewis is shown as a Grand Rapids Police officer wearing the white cap of a "corner cop." He was directing traffic in this scene from the '30s. He preferred police work to that of firemen because he "didn't like sitting all day."

PHOTO/Courtesy Nancy Van'tHof

Just a few weeks after Orson Welles frightened the public with his radio adaptation of "War of the Worlds," and with evil rumors coming from Germany, the holiday season got off to a hopeful start on Nov. 19, 1938, with the annual Christmas Parade on Monroe Avenue at Ottawa in downtown Grand Rapids. The annual parade was sponsored by Wurzburg's Department Store. The Toyland theme was certainly the delight of all the children in the crowd.

PHOTO/Courtesy Grand Rapids Public Library

Now here's a dashing school band in their capes, all made by their moms, according to Max Doering, who is seated at the far left. He played the baritone for the Dickinson School Band in 1935. He still plays, too. Max had a fine career as a stockbroker in Grand Rapids.

PHOTO/Courtesy Max Doering

Ten Dykstra kids pose on their front porch at 1051 Wealthy St. SE in 1931. This wouldn't be the last of them, though. Parents John and Janna would add four more over the next few years. In the back from left: Herman holding baby Frank, Peter, Janna and Barney. In the front from left: Betty, Alida, Julia, John and Boreas.

PHOTO/Courtesy Andrea Snyder

"Why don't ya come over to the Regent and see me, sometime?" In April 1935, clever movie promoters hired a rickshaw and a Mae West look-alike to publicize the actress' latest movie, "Goin' to Town," appearing at the Regent Theater.

PHOTO/Courtesy Grand Rapids Public Library

Happy to be photographed in the goat wagon is Stanford Brown of the northwest side of Grand Rapids. Photo 1933.

PHOTO/Courtesy Norma Corby

The American Bakery Co. was the forerunner of the present-day American Bread Co. In the 1930s, it was located on Bridge Street. Here, driver/salesman Ed "Red" Zyniewicz poses by his trusty van, old No. 6.

PHOTO/Courtesy Thomas J. Zyniewicz

1940s

The Camp Fire Girls Drum & Bugel Corps. greets the arrival of the Red Feather Train in 1948. A trio of Boy Scouts were on hand as a color guard. The Red Feather Train brought Community Chest representatives from around Michigan to Grand Rapids for a fund raising event at the Civic Auditorium.

PHOTO/Courtesy Wenda Fore

Coach Dan Nameth, far right, is shown with his 1947 Central High School basketball team. Nameth, who later became an official, died of a heart attack while refereeing a football game at Houseman Field in 1962. Since then, the West Michigan Officials Association has honored high school athletes who exhibit high standards in their sport and in the classroom, and exemplify good sportsmanship and community service with the Nameth Award.

PHOTO/Courtesy Don Boeskool

What a mess. A fire on May 13, 1949, destroyed the Nichols & Cox Lumber Co. at 1035 Godfrey Ave. SW. Walter Eavey, a neighbor, was hosing his garage hoping the flames would not come his way. This photo was taken from his back yard. The curious are looking at the aftermath of the blaze.

PHOTO/Courtesy Walter Eavey

Bill Lewis, 5, is about to suffer an ignomy that many young men of his age have endured. He must wear clothes that his mother picked out for his first day of school in 1940. And he hated short pants, says his daughter, Lisa Koster. "He was the only kid wearing them, but his mom worked at Steketee's, had already purchased the outfit and made him wear it." Bill braved it through and eventually made a nice career for himself with the Postal Service. Not as a mail carrier, though, which might have seen him wear shorts again.

PHOTO/Courtesy Lisa Lewis Koster

Nurses Jean Norton, left, Norma McManus and Betty Miller are outside Saint Mary's Hospital for a photo in 1944.

PHOTO/Courtesy Kathy Scheer

Charlotte VanderVeen poses by the rock in front of South High School in June 1946. This was on the corner of Hall Street and Jefferson Avenue.

PHOTO/Courtesy Charlotte Geelhoed

The C. S. Raymer Well Drilling Co. is busy outside the Rowe Hotel (now the empty Olds Manor) on Michigan Street NE circa 1939.

PHOTO/Courtesy Gerry Neubecker

During the mid-40s and into the early '50s, the All American Girls Professional Baseball League provided baseball action while the young men were serving in the armed forces. In Grand Rapids, the Chicks were the local franchise, from 1945 to 1954. This photo, from about 1947, shows, from left: Twila Shively, Inez "Lefty" Voyce, Manager John Rawling, Ruth "Tex" Lessing and Connie Wisniewski. The Chicks were league champs in 1948 and in 1953, when they won in the last inning of the last game over the Kalamazoo Lassies. Chicks' pitcher "Beans" Risinger struck out Doris Sams, one of the best hitters in the league, on a 3-2 count with the bases loaded to end the game. Nancy O'Rear, who provided this photo, was too young to play for the team, but faithfully kept a scrapbook of news clippings of every game and story about her beloved Chicks.

PHOTO/Courtesy Nancy Kellogg O'Rear

Gordon Food Service employees are shown in front of a company
warehouse at 320 State St. SE, in the late 1940s. The business was begun
in 1897 by 23-year-old Isaac VanWestenbrugge, a Dutch immigrant,
who borrowed $300 from his older brother, Martin, to start a business
delivering butter and eggs in Grand Rapids. The company is now the
largest family-owned and operated food distributor in North America.

PHOTO/Courtesy Kathy Perry/Gordon Food Service

Frank Chrystler, an engineer for the Grand Rapids Fire Department, Engine Co. No. 6 at Ellsworth and Grandville avenues, is pictured in a fire truck about 1943. He served with the company from 1914 to 1943.

PHOTO/Courtesy Sherry VanOeveren Bouwman

Coach Schrump and the lads of the 1940 Creston High School football team pose for a team photo. Joey Noorthoek, No. 50, second row third from left, was named an All City/All State player.

PHOTO/Courtesy Noorthoek Family

Bill Mahoney of Grand Rapids served in the Army Air Corps in Manilla, Phillipines during World War II. His father, William L. Miller, worked for Consumers Power Co. on Pearl Street. Bill, who was one of five children, studied engineering at Michigan State University and after the war moved to California where he worked for Kaiser Motors. He is shown in combat readiness about 1943.

PHOTO/Courtesy Ruth Miller

Young Joe Podell is seen on his Grand Rapids Press carrier route in 1948. Joe went on to a 44-year career in sales and marketing for The Press and for Booth Newspapers.

PHOTO/Courtesy Joe Podell

In 1946, the Grand River decided to expand its boundaries and bedevil riverside property owners and businesses. This view from the west side shows the Hotel Pantlind in the upper right across the river. The Bissell Carpet Sweeper building is at the far left.

PHOTO/Courtesy Henry Zeman

For many years, Billie Pratt Wright operated a restaurant/variety store at 1106 Chicago Drive SW. Born in Chicago, Billie hawked papers on the city's south side and later taught elementary school and ran restaurants in Detroit and New York City. She moved to Grand Rapids in 1930 when her second husband bought the building at Chicago Drive and turned it into the Urbandale Restaurant. Al Capone and Henry Ford were among those said to have known Billie. The place operated as a restaurant until its conversion to a variety store. Billie, by then nearly blind and partly deaf, sold the place in 1977 and died in 1979.

PHOTO/Courtesy Terrel Grooters

Giving the photographer a wide smile is Julia Zigmont on her way to St. Peter & Paul School on Quarry Avenue NW in 1947.

PHOTO/Courtesy Norma Corby

Having staked out a prime spot on the sidewalk, these youngsters were awaiting the start of the July 4th parade on Monroe Avenue in 1946. From left: Barbara Downer (Bowe), Roger and Teddy Barecki, Arlene Downer (Patterson) and Roman Downer. Barbara is current president of the Santa Claus Girls charity.

PHOTO/Courtesy Roman Downer

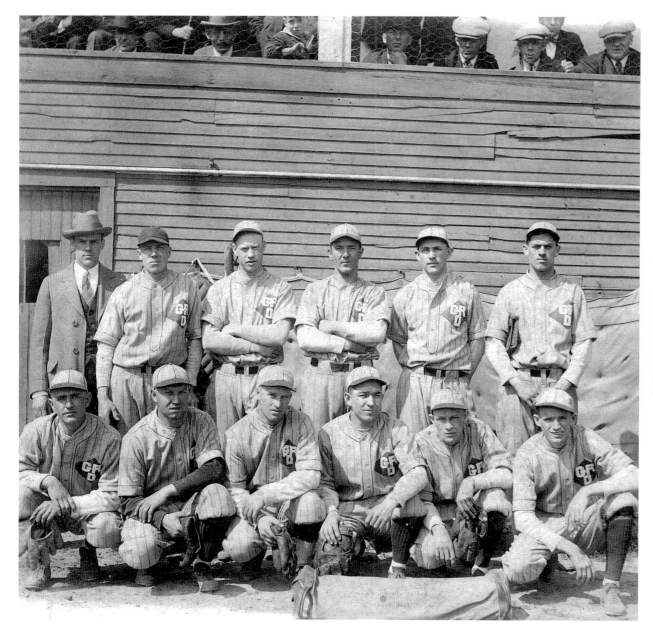

The Grand Rapids "somethings," because the last name is unreadable on the bat bag in front of the team, are shown preparing for a game at Valley Field in 1945.

PHOTO/Courtesy Barbara Sue Damore

Out for a day of fun at Ramona Park in 1944 are James, Colleen and Hannah Barr. Their dad, Fred, just happened to manage the park at the time, so they got the best cars. Hannah's, in fact, is supercharged.

PHOTO/Courtesy Colleen (Barr) Van Putten

High school kids in the late '40s and '50s at South High favored Joppe's Ice Cream as a place to hang out and meet friends. Gasper Amodeo, right, worked there for two years before he graduated in 1950, doing everything from waiter to cook to busboy. Rita Gibbs is at left. The photo dates from 1948. Joppe's was on the corner of Jefferson Avenue and Hall Street SE.

PHOTO/Courtesy Gasper Amodeo

The Haskelite Company was proud of its bowling team, the Haskelite Mystics. In 1946, the team included Nancy (Hall) Krenz, 19, at far right.

PHOTO/Courtesy Krenz Family

You wouldn't want this bunch on your tail. The men of the Grand Rapids Police Motorcycle Division definitely look like they mean business. The squad lined up for a photo at John Ball Park in 1947. Among them, eighth from left, is Lewis Vander Meer who, at 91, is the only man pictured who is still living at the time of this book's publication. Lewis, who was the first World War II draftee from Grand Rapids, retired from the force in 1976 as a major and chief of detectives. Charles Harshberger took the photo.

PHOTO/Courtesy Lewis Vander Meer

Though delivery was delayed a couple years by World War II, the Grand Rapids Fire Department was at last pleased to take delivery of a new 100-foot ladder truck in September 1947. The truck cost $25,000 and was later dedicated to a former fireman, Clair W. Evans, who was killed in action while serving the nation in the European theater of war.

PHOTO/Courtesy Robert Imhoff

Dressed as "kinderen," Geraldine and Arthur Van Houten take time out from various mischief to pose for a photo taken by their mother, Coby, in 1940 in the backyard of their home at 1123 Lee St. off Godfrey Avenue SW.

PHOTO/Courtesy Coby Van Houten

Wartime romance blossomed between Anne Mahoney and John Christian, who were pictured at the Mahoney home on 1141 Lake Drive in 1943. The couple was married shortly before John shipped out to serve in Germany. Anne, whose father, William L. Miller, worked for Consumers Power Co. on Pearl Street, was one of five Mahoney children. She later joined the Women's Army Auxillary Corps and served in Texas. After the war, the couple moved to Chicago briefly and then to Providence, R.I.

*PHOTO/Courtesy
Ruth Mahoney Miller*

The Central Reformed Church, corner of Fountain Street and Barclay Avenue, as it appeared with a blanket of snow in the late 1940s. It would later be destroyed in a 1953 fire. (See photo, page 159.)

PHOTO/Courtesy Central Reformed Church

Proud of their brother are Adrianna, left, and Mary DeBruyn. Marinus was preparing to ship off for World War II duty in 1942 as a naval signal man.

PHOTO/Courtesy Mary Nozal

A view of the Sixth Street dam looking west shows a fisherman or two, and maybe a swimmer, in the Grand River below the dam in this photo from the 1940s. The photographer may have perched on the Belknap area ridge to take the shot. The west side canal is still in place, but no fish ladder...yet.

PHOTO/Courtesy Henry Zeman

Once upon a time, fellow classmates did the honor of helping you cross the street to school. In 1941, the entire cadre of crossing guards at Congress School posed for a portrait. Among them was one Don Boeskool, second row, far left. It's a good-looking, friendly crew who likely discharged their responsibilities with diligence.

PHOTO/Courtesy Don Boeskool

These two are obviously plotting some mischief. Brothers Gordon, left, and Bill Wing were playing at the family home at 848 Dallas Ave. SE, when the boys' father, Harold, took this shot in 1949. Gordon, in the sailor's cap, has an official Roy Rogers cap gun. The Roadmaster (we think) bike is outfitted with a sizeable headlamp for daring exploits after dark.

PHOTO/Courtesy Bill Wing

Now here's a scene familiar to thousands, at least, of Grand Rapids families – a shot of a youngster perched happily on the lap of the statue of John Ball in John Ball Park. Originally from New Hampshire, Ball came to the area as a land agent for East Coast investors. He served 21 years on the school board and was elected to the state legislature. He donated 40 acres of land that formed the park bearing his name at Fulton Street and Valley Avenue SW. He died in 1884. The statue was unveiled in 1925 and has been a favorite of children since. Keeping the tradition alive in this 1942 photo are Alfred and Jennie Harvey and their daughter, Janice. The two bronze kids on Ball's lap are his grandchildren, Virginia and her cousin, Albert.

PHOTO/Courtesy Mike Harvey

She was a senior at Union High School in 1942, but Rose Marie Blain was good enough on the bassoon to play with the Grand Rapids Symphony, which she did for two years. You can spot Miss Blain just to the left of the piano in the background. The conductor was Nickoli Milco.

PHOTO/Courtesy
Rose Marie Blain

In the early 1940s, John and Betty Shirley pose for a photo in happier times. John would later be killed in World War II and American Legion Post 384 would be named in his honor.

PHOTO/Courtesy Tim Sabo

Ah, those Shriners, they know how to party on New Year's Eve. Glen and Mille Blandford have some fun with cardboard cutouts at the Masonic Temple on Fulton Street in this 1945 photo. Glen's younger brother, Vic, founded the Blandford Nature Center.

PHOTO/Courtesy Ben Blandford

Fun times with Spike nearly didn't happen for Catherine Haney and her brother, Donald, back in 1946. Seems their mom was opposed to them taking in the stray dog and ordered him back to the pound, recalls Catherine. That upset Donald, who couldn't, or wouldn't, eat. So, back to the pound the family went and now paid a buck or two to retrieve the pooch, which promptly bit Donald on his first day back home. Things settled down after that, Catherine says, and her brother hitched Spike up to a make-shift wagon to pull his little sister. "Boy, if that dog saw a cat, it became one wild ride," she said. *PHOTO/Courtesy Catherine Haney*

Paul Wright is pictured in front of his service station, 1125 Burton St. SW in Wyoming Township, about 1940, on a slow business day. Across the street was a little place called Terry's Sandwich Shop. According to information that accompanied the photo, Mr. Wright was the fifth husband of Billie Wright who ran "Billie's Variety" on Chicago Drive and Godfrey Avenue SW.

PHOTO/Courtesy Terrel Grooters

Jack Steed, son of Clayton Steed, co-owned Steed Pharmacy on the corner of Palmer Street and Coit Avenue. Clayton purchased the store in 1927. Ellen Davis was the friendly counter clerk.

PHOTO/Courtesy Steed Family

"My dad caught the trout, but there I am taking the credit," says Floyd Hocum of this handsome catch landed by his dad from the Grand River in 1947. Their home was at 966 S. Division Ave.

PHOTO/Courtesy Floyd Hocum

1940s

127

Sisters Orlene and Betty Shirley are having some fun shopping downtown on Monroe Avenue in this 1940s shot. During this period, roving photographers would often snap candid shots and then offer them for sale. Grand Rapids papparazzi?

PHOTO/Courtesy Tim Sabo

Helping dad (Erwin Sullivan) in the Victory Garden is young John Sullivan. Vegetables may not have been a favorite just yet with the wee lad. The family lived at 210 Griggs St. SE.

PHOTO/Courtesy John Sullivan

Photographed in November 1944, Union High School grads and friends Burton Bouwkamp, left, and James Van Oosten are shown ready for service in World War II. Burt, Union's Class of 1944 vice president, was home on his first leave from the Navy. Jim, Union's Class of 1944 president, entered the Army in January 1945. Forty years later, Jim was president of Rose-Johnson Furniture Company in Grand Rapids and Burt was head of Chrysler's Japan operations in Tokyo.

PHOTO/Courtesy Burt Bouwkamp

Proud of his country, young Richard Timmerman
salutes the flag at his grandparents' house,
Garfield Avenue and First Street, in this photo
from the early 1940s. The house was later razed
to make room for Int. 196.

PHOTO/Courtesy Andrea Snyder

Books are open, hair is combed and ribbons in place – one young lady is even wearing a
necklace – and thus, the scholars of Cummings School, kindergarten through sixth grade in one
room, had their photo taken in Feburary 1946. Young Dave Van Oostendorp is on the far right
side, fourth row back.

PHOTO/Courtesy Dave Van Oostendorp

It was a proud moment for Frank Pierce as he received the Medal of Honor from Pres. Harry Truman in June 1948. Pierce, who was a Navy corpsman during World War II, was awarded the nation's highest military honor for saving wounded Marines during the Battle of Iwo Jima. Pierce later spent about 35 years with the Grand Rapids Police Department, ascending to acting chief before retiring in the early 1980s. He died of cancer in 1986, at age 62. In 2004, toymaker Hasbro added the Frank Pierce action figure to its line of Medal of Honor soldiers.

PHOTO/Courtesy Paula Pierce

In 1925, Herman Baker arrived in America from the Netherlands with other members of his family. He worked for several years in his uncle Louis Kregel's bookstore, primarily in the used-book department, which consisted mostly of theological volumes. In 1932, he married Angeline Sterkengberg. In 1939, Baker, 28, purchased the building in this photo (ca. 1946), 1019 Wealthy St., and with some shelves built by a friend, two used desks and a typewriter purchased from a Salvation Army store, went to work. The rent was $18 a month. Baker later became an active leader in the area's Calvin Christian Reformed Church, and a leader in the Christian school movement. The little company has grown to encompass Baker Publishing Group, which has partnerships with several Christian publishing companies.

PHOTO/Courtesy Dave Baker

Mary Reynolds, 16, seated, is shown with a friend at a tennis tournament. She loved playing at Garfield Park. A note on the back of the photo says "I'm that 'cute' kid sitting on the bench – just in case I don't recognize myself when I'm in my old age."

PHOTO/Courtesy Deb Moore

On the primary trail in 1948, candidate Gerald R. Ford, right, visited with farmers in Paris Township, where he promised to milk their cows if he won. Well, he won, so the young man returned to keep his promise. From left are Royal Patterson, Fred Darling and Melvin Patterson. You could always count on Gerry, eh?

PHOTO/Courtesy The Grand Rapids Press Archives

The Berkey & Gay Furniture plant No. 2 on Monroe Avenue NW met a fiery end in November 1943. One firefighter, Louis Coleman, was killed by a falling wall during the blaze.

PHOTO/Courtesy Robert Imhoff

Janna Dykstra's brother, Pete, recently bought a camera and encouraged his sister to strike her best movie star pose for him. The photo was taken at their home on Sigsby Street in the early 1940s.

PHOTO/Courtesy Pete Dykstra

A good soda fountain was the place to meet friends and hang out in the late 1940s. Dutmers Drug Store in East Grand Rapids on Wealthy Street at Lovett Avenue was a good one. Some friends ham it up for the camera in this late 1940s shot. Rose's popcorn and caramel corn were sold here, too.

PHOTO/Courtesy Dorothy (Kruizenga) Alderton

Doing his best Bing Crosy is Bernard Sielawa of Grand Rapids, who was an auto mechanic for Nash Chevrolet, now Classic Chevrolet. Bernard, whose father immigrated from Poland in the early 1900s, was a first-generation American.

PHOTO/Courtesy Christine Kris

The Bolthouse family – Peter and Leona, and daughters, Joyce (back) and Audrey – are looking at a Grand Rapids Press with headlines announcing the end of World War II. Reason enough for a smiling family photo. The family lived at 1734 Nelson Ave. SE.

PHOTO/Courtesy Joyce I. Bolthouse

It was hay baling day at the Doezema Farm in 1945 when the photographer caught this action. Charles Persenair is driving the tractor, Ken Doezema is operating the baler.

PHOTO/Courtesy Doezema Family

A dozen ladies sorting. In this circa 1945 photo, Laurence Makus of the U.S. Postal Service finds himself supervising the training of a host of young women in new jobs at the Grand Rapids Post Office.

PHOTO/Courtesy Amy Kosta

Lester A. Kennedy finds himself the lone dispatcher on the desk at the Grand Rapids Police Department in this 1940s-era photo. Lester and his wife, Elizabeth, lived on Beechwood Street NE in a home they purchased for $400. The couple reared four children. Handyman Lester restored both the interior and the exterior of the family home.

PHOTO/Courtesy Mary Borrello

Ready for day's sail on Reeds Lake in the summer of '44 are three pretty sailors from East Grand Rapids. Janet Russell, left, Joan Martin and Marcia Travis are set to depart the Grand Rapids Yacht Club dock... as soon as they untie that last line attached to a cleat on the dock.

PHOTO/Courtesy Grand Rapids Public Library

One of the family flicks showing in July 1943 was "My Friend Flicka," starring Roddy McDowall. You could have watched it at the Majestic Theater on the corner of Division Avenue and Library Street. The building is now the home of the Grand Rapids Civic Theatre.

PHOTO/Courtesy Grand Rapids Public Library

Horse-drawn delivery for Grand Rapids Creamery was coming to a close when this photo was taken in 1949, as the company went to motorized trucks the very next year, according to Bill Wing whose father, Harold, is the snappy delivery man. Harold began working for the company in 1925 and retired in 1964. Eight-year-old Bill snapped this photo in front of the family house at 848 Dallas Ave. SE. "My dad would come home for lunch and my mom would make him clean up after the horse," Bill recalled. "She didn't like the piles it left behind."

PHOTO/Courtesy Bill Wing

It was 1943, and while the war raged on in other parts of the world, folks at home did what they could. In this photo, employees of the General Motors Fisher Body Plant on 36th Street are shown during a live Victory Garden radio program on WOOD radio. From left are Austin Hartwell, Mr. Kilmer and Martin Starr. The fellow with his back to the camera is an unidentified WOOD radio host. The Hartwell family did raise a Victory Garden, according to Austin's son, Richard.

PHOTO/Courtesy Richard Hartwell

This happy young couple, Edward and Carroll Doran, were photographed outside a restaurant on Division Avenue near Burton Heights in May 1947.

PHOTO/Courtesy Doran Family

1940s

In November 1949, a local event called "Grand Rapids on Parade" showcased locally-made goods. This photo of the Fox Deluxe Brewing Company booth shows the brewer's best products. Fox Deluxe was a popular brew... so we've heard.

PHOTO/Courtesy
Grand Rapids Public Library

1950s

Patrolman Bill Wilfred Conrad looks to the safety of pedestrians and drivers at the busy Campau Square intersection in this 1956 photo. Conrad was often called the "Cop on the Corner." He and several other patrolmen were know by the police department as "cornermen." He was with the police force for 20 years, retiring in 1963. *PHOTO/Courtesy Conrad Family*

There he is. Mr. Richard Nixon stumping for re-election as Vice President of the United States in Grand Rapids in 1956. The photo was taken by Bert Boerema Jr.

PHOTO/Courtesy Trudy Boerema Fetters

Six-year-old buckaroo Tom Julien beams from the saddle of Thunder the palamino as his cowboy hero and the horse's owner, Buck Barry, holds the reins. Buck had a long running Saturday morning show called "Buckaroo Rodeo" (1953-1969) on WOOD-TV, where he would sing, play guitar and spin a lariat. Children in the audience would ride a wooden bronco and raced in relays atop wooden horses. Buck also visited sick children in hospitals and made guest appearances at Halloween parties and Easter egg hunts. In 1987, he served as grand marshal for the Grande Centennial Celebration parade in Grand Rapids. He passed away in El Paso, Texas in 1997.

PHOTO/Courtesy Carole McKernan

Barbara Hamilton Bearinger is working on a mangle, an ironing machine, in this 1956 photo. Many housewives owned and operated this device. A electric mangle had a rotating padded drum that revolved against a heating element. Laundry fed into the turning mangle emerged flat and pressed on the other side. Voila.

PHOTO/Courtesy Barbara Sue Damore

It's tough work being a kid. – all that playing. So, a few of the neighbor lads got together for a lunch break on a fine September day in 1950 at Johnny Sullivan's house, 210 Griggs St. SE. Johnny is third from right.

PHOTO/Courtesy John Sullivan

William F. Drueke, who owned William F. Drueke & Sons (maker of wooden board games), was an amateur photographer. In 1958, he took this shot of the Grand Rapids skyline looking east.

PHOTO/Courtesy Mary Kay Groening

The setting is Monkey Island at John Ball Zoo. The year, 1950. Gene, left, and Patti Wisner were not stranded there, rather, they managed to sneak in for a quick photo while the island was under construction – well before the monkey's were let loose.

PHOTO/Courtesy Patti Thomas

Rauser's Sausage store is shown on Bridge Street at Stocking Avenue in the late 1950s. The building is the site of the Little Mexico restaurant, which burned down in September 2008 as this book was in production. The owner plans to rebuild.

PHOTO/Courtesy S.J. King

Wayne's World of Trains. A steam locomotive, a 4-6-2, of the Grand Trunk & Western line, is shown as it was switching a mail car near the engine house on Leonard Street and Plainfield Avenue. Wayne Weers, who photographed the engine, says he grew up on the west side of the city and was always down by the tracks to watch the trains. Once or twice, an engineer even let him ride in the cab. Most steam engines have been gone since the early 1960s. A year after Wayne took this photo in 1957, he entered the service. The recruiter promised him a slot in "transportation," where he could learn to drive the big trains. Instead, they sent him to truck driving school. Wayne drove trucks for 40 years after the service, retiring from Padnos. But his love of trains never diminished.

PHOTO/Courtesy Wayne Weers

She was Queen in 1951 and had a lovely smile to share. Marian Harkens worked in one of 12 Dodgson's Beauty Salons. Each year, owner Glenwood Dodgson hosted an annual parade and picnic for his staff. A "best" hairdresser was chosen from each salon and one of them chosen queen. Marian was about 18 years old. The salon where she worked was near the Van Andel Arena.

PHOTO/Courtesy Stan and Marian Szudera

Peter B. Compaan owned Creston Pet & Garden Supplies at 1823 Plainfield Ave. NE. It was called "The store with the real monkey behind the counter." The monkey, Jo-Jo, was a big hit with customers. Peter and his pal were well-known. He had birds, guinea pigs, and rats. Peter, who had three daughters, later worked for Montgomery Wards and Keeler Brass.

PHOTO/Courtesy Carole Compaan Mieras

Ready for patrol. Motorcycle Patrolmen Frank Pierce, left, Albert Van Dyke, Robert Woronko and Richard Ottenwess are pictured on their bikes in 1953.

PHOTO/Courtesy Marcia Van Dyke

What is it, Lassie? You say you want to visit Grand Rapids and receive the key to the city? You go, girl. Lassie, the famous TV canine did, indeed, get the key to the city and was photographed with the item at the Kent County Airport about 1955.

PHOTO/Courtesy
Grand Rapids Public Library

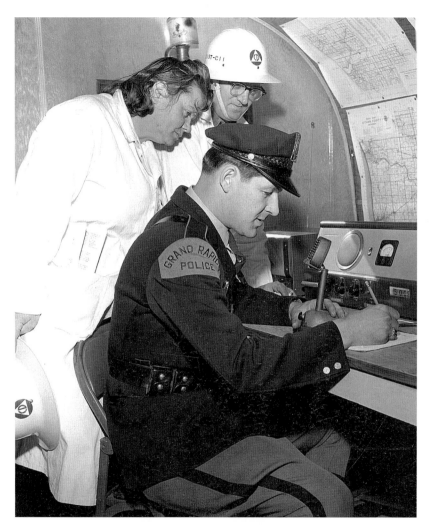

About one month after the devastation of the deadly April 1956 tornado that ripped through Hudsonville, Standale and Comstock Park, the Sector C11 Civil Defense Network thought it should sharpen its skills and set up several practice drills. In this photo, Gert and Al Baker peer over the shoulder of an unidentified patrolman who is sharing information over what was then a pretty high-tech set up. Al was deputy CD warden and Gert was in communications.

PHOTO/Courtesy George Davis/Wing Collection

C'mon, Mary, crank it up! With her husband, Arthur, at the wheel, Mary Doering poses at the crank of a 1910 Model T. Arthur was giving kids rides for a nickel at a Brookside PTA fundraiser in May 1958. She and Arthur participated in Woodland Antique Car Tour events for nearly 50 years.

PHOTO/Courtesy Mary Doering

No big screens? Not yet anyway. In this photo from the early 1950s, the latest television sets from Sylvania are arranged in a display for the Herpolsheimer's department store. The photo was taken by Weston G. Lehr, who designed many of the displays for the popular department store.

PHOTO/Courtesy Ken Mazie

Flowing banners and the state emblem of the Netherlands decorated the Herpolsheimer's department store at Monroe Street and Division Avenue in 1952. The activity was all part of the excitement generated by a visit to the area by the Netherland's Queen Julianna. The photo was taken by Weston G. Lehr, who designed many of the displays for the popular department store.

PHOTO/Courtesy Ken Mazie

Martha Prusak, left, Don Mattone and Mary Schneider perform at an annual recital at The Music Center, 665 Bridge St. NW. The Music Center was serious about its work. It advertised that "You cannot afford to trifle with your child's music education."

PHOTO/Courtesy
Mary Ohm

Beating the heat was no problem for Carl and Paula Groening. A washtub worked just fine on this hot summer day in 1955 at 57 Quigley St. SW.

PHOTO/Courtesy Connie Groening

Looking just a little like Maytag repairmen, this group of Grand Rapids Parks Department caretakers posed for a group shot in the early '50s at the Public Service building at 301 Market St., just south of downtown. These good fellows were responsible for all the parks in the Grand Rapids area.

PHOTO/Courtesy Gary Swets

With polar bears already playing in their spot behind them, workmen ready the otter habitat at the John Ball Zoo in 1959. Jack Swets is standing behind surveyor Carl Wright. Creston High School students were involved in raising funds for the polar bears.

PHOTO/Courtesy Gary Swets

The young ladies of 1108 Lake Michigan Drive thought that a doll show would be an ideal activity one summer afternoon. Carole McKernan, 8, is at the back, far right. "I wish I could remember what doll was mine, but we had a great time," she says.

PHOTO/Courtesy Carole McKernan

Carl, Chris and Paula Groening had some fun on the train at John Ball Zoo on a summer's day in 1955. The kids, and parents, Carl and Constance, lived at 57 Quigley St. SW.

PHOTO/Courtesy Connie Groening

Private parties and picnics throughout Grand Rapids in the late 1940s and 1950s got their baked beans, salads and cole slaw from Boeskool's Home Made Foods. Gerald and Elmira Boeskool started the business after World War II ended. They also sold to grocery stores in the greater Grand Rapids area. The photo dates to about 1950.

PHOTO/Courtesy Don Boeskool

 1950s

151

TORNADO FUNNEL 7:08 P.M.
APR. 3 '56 GEO. DAVIS.

The April 3, 1956 tornado that caused devastation and loss of life in Hudsonville, Standale and Comstock Park was captured on film by local photographer George Davis. The storm was ranked as an F5, the highest category of destructive force for a tornado. The twister claimed 17 lives and caused an estimated $83 million in damage in today's dollars.

PHOTO/Courtesy George Davis/Wing Collection

Jeanne Sloane and daughter, Kathy, pose with her husband, Jim's, racecar in 1955. He raced at the Speedrome in Comstock Park. The track, on North Park Street between the North Park Bridge and West River Drive, opened in 1950 and hosted racing through 1966. It was torn down to make way for the U.S. 131 expressway.

PHOTO/Courtesy Kathy Sloane Wortman

It was a grand summer day in 1954 when the first jet plane to visit Kent County touched down at the old Kent County Airport on 32nd Street SE. Young and old alike (guests were limited to those who worked for Civil Defense, police and fire departments) came out to see the military wonder and peer into the cockpit of a hot new F-89 Scorpion, a fighter-interceptor. Several of the planes were making goodwill tours of airports in the country. An Air Force pilot perched on the wing, far left, answered questions about the plane. *PHOTO/Courtesy Harold and Bill Wing*

Early in the past century, two stately American elm trees had taken up residence on a beautiful hill just east of the river. But progress came along, the city grew up and spread. Bostwick Avenue NE was built, but the road builders had not the heart to destroy the trees, so they went around them. Occasionally, someone would make noises about cutting them down, but the trees survived all attempts until early in 1950, shortly after this photo was taken. They were deemed a traffic hazard and a menace to the homes on the west side of the road.

PHOTO/Courtesy
Grand Rapids Public Library

William F. Drueke, who owned William F. Drueke & Sons (maker of wooden board games), was an amateur photographer. In 1958, he took this shot of the Bridge Street bridge looking east. The U.S. Post office now occupies the left, site of the former Grand Trunk Railroad depot. The DeVos Place convention center is now on the right.

PHOTO/Courtesy Mary Kay Groening

Capt. Marvin Ford served in the Grand Rapids Fire Department for more than 35 years.

PHOTO/Courtesy JoEllen Ford Nickles

You're next! Harry G. Brummel, center, was one of the smiling sartorial experts who kept men neat and groomed from the McKay Tower Barber Shop. This photo is from 1955. He retired about 1957. His father, Harry R. Brummel, was also a barber, much earlier in the century.

PHOTO/Courtesy
Harry Brummel

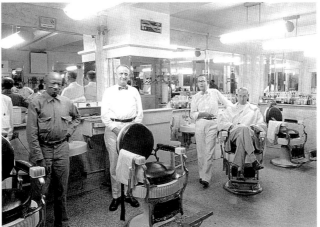

1950s

GRAND RAPIDS HERALD CARRIERS
WASHINGTON, D. C. APRIL 1955

Here it was, April 1955 and already a bunch of stuff had happened. In January the Pentagon announced a plan to develop intercontinental ballistic missiles armed with nuclear weapons. The Soviet Union decided to officially end its war with Germany. In February, the seventh fleet of the United States Navy helped the Republic of China evacuate the Chinese Nationalist army and residents from Tachen Islands to Taiwan. NBC produced the Mary Martin Peter Pan show, the first time that a stage musical was presented in its entirety on TV exactly as performed on stage. The song "Rock Around the Clock" by Bill Haley and his Comets helped make Rock and Roll a musical genre. Winston Churchill resigned as Prime Minister of the United Kingdom. Richard J. Daley was elected mayor of Chicago. The Salk polio vaccine was introduced in April and in the same month Ray Kroc opened a McDonald's fast food restaurant. So, by the time these veteran Grand Rapids Herald carriers hit the streets of Washington D.C. for a visit, the capital was already hoppin. The lads won the trip by obtaining a certain number of new customers on their route.

PHOTO/Courtesy Al Kowalczyk

Ramona Park in East Grand Rapids adjacent to Reeds Lake had a wonderful amusement park from 1879-1955. Its wooden roller coaster was one of the best. Richard Kruizenga took this shot at the top of the coaster and managed to hang onto the camera to get the film developed. (Circa 1950).

PHOTO/Courtesy Richard Kruizenga Sr.

The fine crew of the Grand Rapids Fire Department No. 5 Pumper Co. pose for a photo in 1950. No. 5 was at the corner of Monroe Avenue and Leonard Street. In the front row, second from right, is Joe Rutka.

PHOTO/Courtesy Judy Rutka-Froedtert

It was a really big shew, er, show, in Grand Rapids when Ed Sullivan came to town for a Herpolsheimer's promotion in the early '50s. The store was giving away a new automobile and Ed took time to pose with a couple of unidentified gentlemen. The photo was taken by Weston G. Lehr, who designed many of the displays for the popular department store.

PHOTO/Courtesy Ken Mazie

Happy days. On Dec. 12, 1953, Alice J. Johnell and David H. Davey said their "I do's" at North Park Presbyterian Church. The couple reared three children – Stewart, Julia and William – and are still members of the church.
PHOTO/Courtesy Barbara Ryman

The Central Reformed Church, corner of Fountain Street and Barclay Avenue NE, as it appeared following a fire that destroyed most of the structure in February 1953. (See picture, page 123.)

PHOTO/Courtesy Central Reformed Church

1950s

All aboard at Ramona Park for a trip around the park on a cool scaled-down steam train. The park operated from 1897-1955 and had steamboat rides, a theater, playgrounds, canoe rentals and carnival rides. Bud Glidden stands next to the engineer, who is known only as Harry.

PHOTO/Courtesy Donna Boelema

A first grade class at Beckwith School looks bright and sharp for the camera. Donna Decker (Lyon) is the third one back on the far left. The teacher's name is not known.

PHOTO/Courtesy Donna Lyon

The Leach family children pose in their Easter finest in 1959, outside the family home at 908 Scribner NW – Dennis, Roger, Bruce, Gary, Roland, Jan, Cheryl and Linda. Mom was pregnant with No. 9, who would be named Julayne.

PHOTO/Courtesy Linda Simard

Enthusiastic skaters enjoy
an evening spin around the
rink in this photo taken at
John Ball Park in the 1950s.

*PHOTO/Courtesy
Henry Zeman*

Nothing like a nice view from above to lend a bit of perspective. The fact that this photo was from about 1950 adds the perspective of time, too. The old Kent County Building, lower left center, and City Hall, lower right, look like some kind of ancient castles by today's standards. The Fox Brewery is at upper left and the Immanuel Lutheran Church at top center. A lot has changed in half a century. *PHOTO/Courtesy Grand Rapids Public Library*

Meijer grocery buyer Charlie Hammet, far right, is shown in the "Home Center" section of the Meijer store, possibly on Leonard Street in this 1950s era photo. The other fellow in the photo is LaVern Hansen. Names of the child and woman are not known.

PHOTO/Courtesy
Evelyn DeShane

Ready for a train ride in May 1958 are Debbie and Johnnie Bek. Their grandfather, Chuck Reynolds, worked for the Pennsylvania Railroad and took the kids for a ride to Holland, along with grandmother, Helen.

PHOTO/Courtesy Deb Moore

Peter Baas, owner of North Park Garage, put together this little assembly for a community parade, recalls his daughter, Linda, the young lass in the dark coat on the trailer. Her sister, Carol, second from left in the back was on hand, too, as was her brother, Gary, standing next to the sign.

PHOTO/Courtesy Linda Van Beek

In town for an "Ice Review" in 1954, Sonja Henie, third from left, is seen with a few friends. Henie is credited with transforming figure skating into a sport and then into popular entertainment. She won Olympic gold in 1928, 1932 and 1936. She shook hands with Adolph Hitler during the 1936 Olympics, was often on the arm of Hollywood star Tyrone Power and threw lavish Hollywood parties. Henie died from leukemia in 1969. Also in the photo are, from left: Lucille Berggren, Gerald Elliott (former Press Editor), Henie, an unknown male, Carol Duvall (who had a long running TV show) and other unknown fellows.

PHOTO/Courtesy Bernard M. Birndorf

This photo of the Silvertone Quartet was taken at the Grand Rapids YMCA on June 6, 1950. The men's names are not known, but they look like a classy group who knew and loved music.

PHOTO/Courtesy Grand Rapids Public Library

The lucky winner of a Sportman's Show promotion picks up her new Nash Rambler station wagon in this March 1951 photo. Delores M. Foote, of 829 S. Ottillia St. SE, receives the keys to her new car from W. Cornell, general manager of the Clock Motor Sales company. It was a low-key affair. Today, there would be all kinds of fanfare and hoopla.

PHOTO/Courtesy Cynthia (Foote) Osenieks

You don't want to go there. The Kent County Jail was at 246 Louis Ave. NW when this photo was taken in 1957. That's a 1955 Chevrolet in the foreground.

PHOTO/Courtesy Roger J. Moll

Bobby socks and saddle shoes were the things to wear for teenage girls in the '50s. In this 1952 photo, eighth grade girls at Immanuel Lutheran School posed for a photo in the school yard at 100 Michigan St. NW. Back, from left: Gila Benz, Rosalind Dorn and Janet Derteen. Front, from left: Joyce and Joan Stoner.

PHOTO/Courtesy Sharon Slabbekoorn

Bill and friends pose outside his Blackstone Cafe, 411 Leonard St. NW, in this early '50s photo. The Budweiser Clydsedale team was making a tour of the area. Must have heard about Bill's great food.

PHOTO/Courtesy Alice Davey

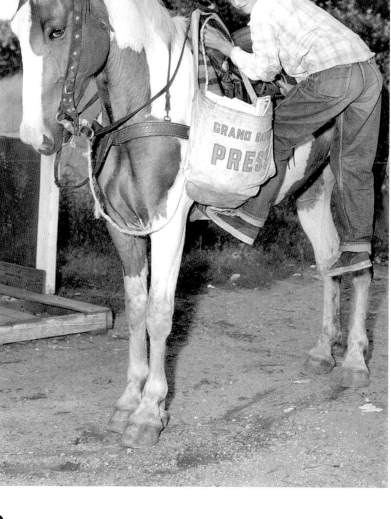

With the price of gas, a portent of the future? Actually, it was 1952 and 14-year-old Robert Yntema was content to deliver papers galloping and trotting over a wide range of territory in southern Kent County on his faithful steed, Trigger. Yes, Trigger. Robert actually saved enough money – $150 – from his route to buy the pinto. He built a stable for Trigger that was attached to the garage of the family home at 5504 Haughey Ave. SW. The family had a collie, too, named Lassie.

PHOTO/Courtesy Robert Yntema

Known to pinch a penny in his day, comedian Jack Benny was the perfect pitchman for a Treasury Department savings bond drive. He's shown in Campau Square during a Liberty Bell Parade in May 1950, shortly after the Liberty Bell replica rang out to signify the opening of the bond drive. Veterans, civic groups and local dignitaries were among those participating in the event.

PHOTO/Courtesy
Grand Rapids Public Library

Mary Jane Russell waves to a photographer as the 1952 Dodgson Beauty Salon parade passes by. For several years, the highest producer from the several Dodgson salons was chosen queen and the next three were her court. The parade started on lower Monroe Avenue, proceeded to Division Avenue and thence to Caledonia Lakeside Park for an annual picnic.

PHOTO/Courtesy Dodgson Realty Co.

While on a date in 1951, sweethearts Nancy Rossman and Ken Bogardus found time for a photograph. He went to Lee High School, she to Union. They have been married for 54 years, have five children, 17 grandchildren and two great-grandchildren. Ken owned RNB Machine and Tool on West River Drive and Nancy worked for Union High School for 20 years.

PHOTO/Courtesy Nancy Rossman Bogardus

Grand Rapids Fire Department personnel Joe Rutka, left, and Andrew Wysocki of the No. 5 Pumper Company, are happy to be involved with Youth Day, a Grand Rapids Press promotion to raise money for news carriers.

PHOTO/Courtesy Judy Rutka-Froedtert

Street scenes give us a sense of how things were and what has changed. This shot from 1952 shows "Dime Store Block" with the H.L. Green, W.T. Grant and F.W. Woolworth stores on Campau Square. Apparently, such stores needed two initials on the marquee.

PHOTO/Courtesy Grand Rapids Public Library

In 1950, Grand Rapids City Commissioner Fred Barr and family posed for a chamber of commerce photo (to be used in a brochure) that touted the local furniture industry. This photo showed that no family was so large that a couch could not be made to accommodate it. From left are: Fred, Brian, Dorothy, Patrick, Bonnie, Terry, Jim, Colleen, Hannah, Fred, Barry and Shannon.

PHOTO/Courtesy Colleen (Barr) Van Putten

Always a hit at the Labor Day Parade – the Nash Kelvinator float with its pretty girls and the latest new appliances. This photo from September 1951 was taken at the corner of Lyon Street and Monroe Avenue. Marilyn DeBoets is on the near side of the range.

PHOTO/Courtesy Marilyn DeBoets

Herman Holmberg, long time furniture design teacher, admires a piece designed at Davis Tech in the 1950s.

PHOTO/Courtesy Carole VandenBerg

1960s

The U.S. 131 S-curve takes form as girders are laid for the road bed in 1960. *PHOTO/Courtesy Richard Skinner*

Cornermen no longer. Five Grand Rapids Police Patrolmen, who were called "cornermen" by the force, were relocated to other duty in 1960. The five had patrolled busy downtown intersections, but such modern traffic aids as "walk and wait" signs, traffic lights, lane signs, turn signs and the like made this duty unnecessary. The five Patrolmen men are, from left: John Stoutjesdyke, Donald Creswell, Arnold DePung, James Moermond and William Conrad.

PHOTO/Courtesy Conrad Family

Thurlow "Ted" DeVlieger, a professional silent movie organist, is shown in a broadcast studio. His granddaughter, Janet Pawloski, believes the photo was taken during the filming of a "TV Mass" at St. Andrews Cathedral in the 1960s. He performed for the TV Mass for 13 years.

PHOTO/Courtesy Janet C. Pawloski

The Nu-Tones were the female equivalent of a barbershop quartet. Shown in 1964, the four ladies were all part of the Grand Rapids chapter of Sweet Adelines. From left: Sally Norton (bass), Arlene Visner (baritone), Jane Schalk (tenor) and Esther Lamoreau (lead).

PHOTO/Courtesy Sally Norton

Smile ladies! It was in the 1960s, but Mary Doering, second from right, and friends fit right into the mood of the Woodland Antique Car Tour event with their circa 1910 costumes. Mary, and her late husband, Arthur, participated in the club for 50 years with several cars.

PHOTO/Courtesy Mary Doering

He won the Valiant! In 1960, a grocery promotion by Starkist offered a new car to lucky winners. Pictured at the Fulton Street market are, from left, the grocery's owner Neal DeYoung; his son, Robert; Henry DeBoer, winner of the car; and Ed Julian. At the wheel of the car, and already with designs on future dates and school dances, is the winner's 15-year-old son, Jim. Hey, coffee was only 69 cents a pound.

PHOTO/Courtesy Jim DeBoer Sr.

Bill Obermeyer is shown sharpening skis in the Bill & Paul's Sporthaus shop in 1965. The shop was then near Lake Drive and Wealthy Avenue SE. Bill loved sailing as did Paul Plasman, owner of the shop (along with Bill Pearson). The two became good friends.

PHOTO/Courtesy John Milhaupt

Rail cars line up in the gypsum mine off Butterworth Avenue SW circa 1965.

PHOTO/Courtesy Henry Zeman

It was a bitter cold day, recalls young patrolman Jon Schutter, left, who was pulled off motorcycle duty to patrol downtown traffic during the busy holiday season in December 1968. His partner is Thomas Schooley. Schutter spent 31 years with the GRPD, working in several capacities, retiring as a lieutenant. The holiday traffic duty was fun, he says, but recalls he lost about 12 pounds even though he ate three big meals a day. A lot of walking. And it got down to 4 below zero on New Year's Eve, he recalled. Cold enough.

PHOTO/Courtesy Jon Schutter

Ah, the Santa Claus shot. On a holiday shopping trip to downtown Grand Rapids in 1969, young Joe Bombul Jr. got to pose with the great man and deliver a well-rehearsed Christmas wish list. Judging by that smile, all went well.

PHOTO/Courtesy Joe Bombul

Sen. Robert F. Kennedy addresses a political gathering at Campau Square on April 11, 1968. 15-year-old Mary Nowak was in the audience and took this snap with her Kodak Instamatic. Less than two months later, Kennedy would be assasinated following a political rally in California.

PHOTO/Courtesy Mary Nowak

Following a summer costume festival for children at Wilcox Park near Aquinas College, the Pulte clan was photographed at their home on the corner of Carol Avenue and Chester Street SE. Don and Colleen's young Indians include, from left, Dean, Mark, Marie, Bill and Don.

PHOTO/Courtesy Don Pulte

It was a whopper. Kevin Patterson, 10, didn't let his limited vision spoil all the fun. So, when the National Trout Contest beckoned in 1960, Kevin and his dad, Lindy Patterson, went out to try their luck at Bear Lake near Kalkaska. The two, who lived at 609 Lafayette Ave., landed a nice rainbow – 23.25 inches and 4.1 pounds – enough for Kevin to win the contest.

PHOTO/Courtesy Shippy Family

Here are the 1963 graduates of St. Peter & Paul School, 1433 Hamilton Ave. NW. *PHOTO/Courtesy Norma Corby*

Lyman J. Bacon taught 7th through 9th grades at Burton Jr. High School. All subjects were fair game for him. He started teaching at this school in the 1940s so he could walk to work. Gas rationing was in effect during the war. This photo dates from 1963.

PHOTO/Courtesy Barbara Bacon

In November 1968, the first E-Unit of the Grand Rapids Police Department hit the road with P. Jager, left, and Bob Cammenga. The two guys are shown checking over supplies before their shift.

PHOTO/Courtesy Robert Cammenga

Fred. J. Barr, left, greets Gov. G. Mennen Williams and Sen. John F. Kennedy, who was on the presidential campaign trail in 1960. Barr was manager of the Civic Auditorium and likely was welcoming the two in advance of a campaign speech.

PHOTO/Courtesy Colleen (Barr) Van Putten

One of West Michigan's first female broadcasters, Dorothy Payne, left, hosted the "Especially for Women" show on WJFM. Asked to be a last-minute substitute, Dorothy did so well she was given a show of her own. She was involved in women's rights and was a member of the Women's Advertising Club, which pushed for a merger with a similar men's group. She later became vice president of media services at J.W. Messner Inc. (Circa 1964).

PHOTO/Courtesy Tracy Payne

One more step and the girl gets it! Actually, these are the Klimek kids who are posing in front of their dad's business van in 1961. He immigrated from Europe with his wife and the kids in 1957. He worked for Expert Coating Co. for 15 years, then bought the company in 1971 and retired in 1991. The four children bought the company in 1991 and still own it. From left: Erik, Patricia, Walter and Menno, the gun hand.

PHOTO/Courtesy Erik Klimek

Giving full voice to a number in a 1963 production of "The Music Man" are the Grand Rapids barber shop quartet known as the Extension Chords. From left, Sid Helder, Cal Verduin, Don Hall and Don Lucas.

PHOTO/Courtesy Sid Helder

One of the last. This photo from the winter of 1960, taken at the Leonard Street and Plainfield Avenue passenger station, shows the last of the Grand Trunk & Western Railroad steam engines. It made runs from Detroit to Muskegon. Steam powered locomotives would largely disappear within just a couple of months of this photo. The number of the train is rather blurry, but could be 5364.

PHOTO/Courtesy Thomas L. Chubinski

These lovely ladies were in the chorus line for a production of "Guys and Dolls" that was performed at Ahavas Israel Synagogue in 1960. Ready to kick up their heels, from left: Sandy Norian, Arlene Cohen, Sue Cohen, Judy Subar and Marcia Bloom.

PHOTO/Courtesy Judy Subar

In 1960, then U.S. Rep. Gerald Ford pinned a medal on the lapel of Inspector Frank Pierce of the Grand Rapids Police Department. Pierce, a recipient of the Medal of Honor for actions in World War II, was given the medal by Ford for helping to train more than 200 members of the 791st Transportation Battalion and 180th Transportation Co., for civil disturbance control. Pierce spent some 35 years with the Grand Rapids Police Department, ascending to acting chief before retiring in the early 1980s. He died of cancer in 1986, at age 62. In 2004, toymaker Hasbro added the Frank Pierce action figure to its line of Medal of Honor soldiers.

PHOTO/Courtesy Paula Pierce

Right around 1959-60, driver's training was held at the Leonard St. Market. Normally a spot to pick up fresh fruits and veggies on Wednesdays and Saturdays, on the other days produce took a back seat to driver's training for Union High School. Mr. Munier, the courageous teacher, is at the right, with Susie Lubinskas at the wheel of what appears to be a Dodge. At far right is Candy May next to Sonia Blough. We wonder why they were wearing smocks.

PHOTO/Courtesy B. Susie Damore

Ready to serve. Recent police recruit graduates salute the flag in this April 1969 commencement ceremony at the Civic Auditorium. The recruits numbered 28 men and one woman, Joanne Sterns, at right, who worked in the juvenile division. It was a time before women were issued uniforms.

PHOTO/Courtesy Dennis Johnson

During a spirited presidential campaign, Richard Nixon had stopped in Grand Rapids for a speech, now it was Sen. Edmund Muskie's turn to make serious noises to the assembled at Campau Square on Nov. 1, 1968. 15-year-old Mary Nowak was in the audience and took this snap with her Kodak Instamatic.

PHOTO/Courtesy Mary Nowak

Charlie Hamment receives congratulations, and a watch, from Hendrik Meijer on the occasion of Charlie's retirement from the Meijer grocery company. Daughter Evelyn DeShane says that her dad was the first grocery buyer for Meijer. Hendrik even signed the photo for Charlie.

PHOTO/Courtesy Evelyn DeShane

In the winter of 1965, the Gerald R. Ford Freeway was dedicated. In attendance were: (between the flag bearers) from left: State Rep. Martin Buth, Richard Ford, James Ford, Co-Committee Chairman Jack Root and State Rep. Thomas Ford.

PHOTO/Courtesy Martin Buth

Hoping for a bite, 9-year-old Larry O'Toole has a line in the water. The outing for handicapped children was sponsored by a local men's group. Later an artist who showed works at various galleries, O'Toole (1951-1986) produced an impressive amount of work despite his battle with childhood rheumatoid arthritis.

PHOTO/Courtesy Lois Whitmore

In late 1961, a shortage of milk jeopardized proper nutrition at children's homes and hospitals in New York City. That did not sit well with George Cope, president of Grocer's Co-op Dairy, who promptly arranged to ship 1,000 half-gallon containers of milk to the Big Apple to ensure the kids were getting their Vitamin D. He's pictured here, at left, with Dave Van Oostendorp, second from left, Lou Munger and an unidentified pilot. Cope began Grocer's Co-op Dairy Co. in 1945 with L.V. Eberhard and others. That company eventually became Country Fresh Inc., from which he retired in 1982.

PHOTO/Courtesy Dave Van Oostendorp

Sen. John Kennedy made a 1960 presidential campaign stop in Grand Rapids. That's our man in the limo, being chauffered to a campaign rally. It was an exciting day, as Kennedy addressed many hundreds of people at the rally.

PHOTO/Courtesy
Grand Rapids Public Library

A smiling Joe Shirley marches in the American Legion Parade in August 1963. Shirley served in the Navy during WWII.

PHOTO/Courtesy Tim Sabo

Len Marzal, center, gives flight instructions to pilot Verne Eady as the men prepare for a business trip. Len was an avid flyer and owned a plane for his engineering business, Rapid Design Services. The photo, from the 1960s, looks to have been taken at the former Kent County Airport on 32nd Street.

PHOTO/Courtesy Arline Dzwonkowski

John Ball has a couple visitors at his station at John Ball Park. Visiting this day in 1969 are Gregory Cook, 7, and his sister, Meredith, 5.

PHOTO/Courtesy Roger Cook

The Saladin Shrine Chanters, outfitted in their best pressed white suits and white shoes, give voice to a number during this event in 1964. The reason for the gathering is not known.

PHOTO/Courtesy Evelyn DeShane

Proud fathers, each with more than 20 years experience on the Grand Rapids Police force, pinned badges on newly certified policemen sons in this April 1969 ceremony. In the foreground, Patrolman Harold Johnson with his son, Dennis; next, Detective Robert Winters needs two hands for his two sons, Robert J. and Dale; and in the rear, Joe Zemaitis pins a badge on his son, James. All the fathers are now gone. Dennis Johnson retired as a sergeant, Robert Winters as a detective, Dale as a lieutenant and James as a patrolman. Dennis, who submitted the photo, said he became good friends with former Press reporter Ed Kotlar who used to ride along on his beat. "I was assigned to the emergency unit for about 18 years and also worked the juvenile beat," he said.

PHOTO/Courtesy Dennis Johnson

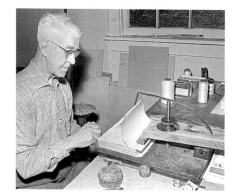

N. L. Rodenhouse was a skilled bookbinder who made the craft a hobby when he retired in 1951. This photo accompanied a 1962 article in The Grand Rapids Press that noted he was the last bookbinder in Grand Rapids. He rebound rare books for the Grand Rapids Public Library and the treasured books of his friends. Here he demonstrates a machine that he designed in 1912 for sewing books before they are covered. He lived at 1045 Oakleigh Road NW, which, for a time, was a treasurehouse of his meticulous work.

PHOTO/Courtesy Marian Grant

A young visitor takes in the heady aroma of fresh roasted coffee beans at the Coffee Ranch on N. Division Avenue in this photo from around 1965. Store owner Arvid Corlin is doing the demonstration. The store is now part of Herman's Boy Inc. in Rockford.

PHOTO/Courtesy Orville Peterson

A view looking west along Crescent Street in January 1965 shows the County Building looming formidably in the distance.

PHOTO/Courtesy Michael Rhoades

Congressman Gerald R. Ford poses with recent graduates from the Grand Rapids Police Academy in January 1966. From left: Patrolman Robert F. Wildman, Superintendent William A. Johnson, Patrolman James Kuipers, Ford, Patrolman David L. Russell, Deputy Superintendent John J. McGavin, Patrolman David Marion and Grand Rapids Mayor Christian H. Sonneveldt.

PHOTO/Courtesy Mr. and Mrs. R. F. Wildman

Hamming it up for the photographer are five-year-old Michelle "Mimi" Karston, left, and her friend Joni Lechtarski, 6. They were posing for a neighborhood friend who just got a camera. The photo dates from 1964 and was taken at 839 McReynolds NW.

PHOTO/Courtesy Michelle Karston

The old and the new. The old City Hall, a Gothic Victorian edifice, was demolished in 1969. The new Kent County Court House is on the site today. In the background, looking west along Lyon Street, is the new Old Kent Bank building – new for the time, anyway. This photo dates from about 1968-69.

PHOTO/Courtesy Mary Forman

The third grade students at St. Alphonsus School in 1959 flex their reading skills for the camera under the watchful eye of Sister Edwarda. Second from left in the second row is Teresa Maksymowski.

PHOTO/Courtesy Mary Maksymowski

Sometime in 1963, Don Kranenberg Jr., left, and his brother, Steve, got to meet Congressman Gerald R. Ford at his office in Washington, D.C. The boy's dad knew Ford through community work and, while on a family vaction in the nation's capital, set up the meeting with Ford. (Later in 1963, Ford would be named to the Warren Commission that would look into the assassination of Pres. John F. Kennedy.)

*PHOTO/Courtesy
Don Kranenberg Sr.*

The entire corps of school crossing guards is shown in their dress uniforms in 1968. At upper left is Officer Bob Gelderbloom, a well-liked safety officer who visited area schools to deliver words of wisdom about safety to the students. In the middle row, third from left, is Sue Harvey, who said Officer Bob was a friendly man who was loved by the kids and his co-workers. Officer Ray Plank, upper right, followed Gelderbloom in the role of safety liaison to area schools. Harvey worked in front of Creston High School crossing students to Palmer Elementary, and later at the intersection of Ann Street and Coit Avenue NE.

PHOTO/Courtesy Sue Harvey

196

1960s

Burgers, the bigger the better, were a hallmark at the Fat Boy Cafeteria at 243 Michigan St. NE. A second Fat Boy served up the calorie-laden treats at 2452 Plainfield Ave. NE. Both are now closed. If it were still there, the Michigan Street Fat Boy would now have as its neighbor the new Fred and Lena Meijer Heart Center.

PHOTO/Courtesy
Grand Rapids Public Library

"Miss Jean" was a favorite with pre-schoolers throughout the area. The engaging host of WOOD-TV's "Romper Room" kept the little ones occupied with stories, games and other activities. This photo of Jean Gordon on the set was taken on June 15, 1960.

PHOTO/Courtesy Grand Rapids Public Library

In 1960, Democratic presidential candidate John F. Kennedy was in town to address a C.I.O. labor union convention. He also appeared outside, addressing a large crowd on Monroe Street at the corner of Pearl Street and Campau Avenue.

PHOTO/Courtesy John Milhaupt

Raymond Edwards served for 30 years in the Grand Rapids Police Department, from 1958-88.

PHOTO/Courtesy Andrea Edwards

Monsignor Hugh Michael Beahan is shown at a broadcast console in the WOOD TV-8 studio in the early 1950s. Beahan was well-known for a long-running TV-8 show called "Fifteen With Father." He also proposed televising the St. Andrew's Mass, which for years he produced and directed. The televised Mass first aired in April 1954. Beahan, known by viewers as "Father Mike," was rector of the cathedral when he died in 1980. The televised Mass ran until March 1997.

PHOTO/Courtesy Janet C. Pawloski

Bibliography

In addition to information provided by PHOTO/Contributors, the following sources were used in the preparation of captions for this volume:

Grand Rapids city directories
Grand Rapids Public Library
Grand Rapids Press archives
Public Museum of Grand Rapids

Vintage Grand Rapids, A Kaleidoscope of Photographs, Volume II, is a product of the efforts of many people, to whom we express our appreciation. Special effort was made to ensure the accuracy of information accompanying these photographs. However, information written on the backs of photos and dates recalled by contributors might not have been exact. For historical accuracy, we welcome corrections and additional information. It will be forwarded to the appropriate libraries and museums. Please write The Grand Rapids Press Marketing Department, 155 Michigan St. NW, Grand Rapids, MI 49503.

Index